Editor
Lorin Klistoff, M.A.

Editorial Manager
Karen Goldfluss, M.S. Ed.

Editor in Chief
Sharon Coan, M.S. Ed.

Cover Artist
Sue Fullam

Art Coordinator
Cheri Macoubrie Wilson

Creative Director
Elayne Roberts

Imaging
James Edward Grace

Product Manager
Phil Garcia

Publishers
Rachelle Cracchiolo, M.S. Ed.
Mary Dupuy Smith, M.S. Ed.

STAND TEST PRACTICE FOR 5TH GRADE

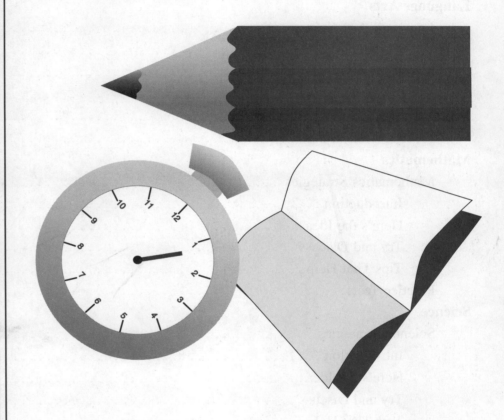

Author

Charles J. Shields

Teacher Created Materials, Inc.
6421 Industry Way
Westminster, CA 92683
www.teachercreated.com
©1999 Teacher Created Materials, Inc.
Made in U.S.A.
ISBN-1-57690-680-9

Table of Contents

You have undoubtedly given plenty of tests during your years of teaching—unit tests, pop quizzes, final exams, and yes, standardized tests. As a professional educator, you know that standardized tests have taken on an importance greater than any of the others.

No one who understands children and the nature of learning would argue that a standardized test provides a measure of a child's understanding, a teacher's effectiveness, or a school's performance. It is a statistical snapshot of a group of children on a particular day. And there is no "generic child." Take a look at a girl named Joanna, for instance. Reluctant to speak during discussions or participate in group work, she's a whiz at taking tests and scores high on formal tests. However, Dion, in the seat beside her, is creative but impulsive. He dawdles during timed tests and sometimes fills in the wrong answer section. His score? It is no more a true indication of his ability than his doodles of motorcycle-riding monsters in the margins of his papers. You are probably thinking of a Joanna or a Dion in your class right now.

However, schools must be accountable to their communities. Moreover, issues of equity and opportunity for children require that some method of checking all students' progress as objectively as possible be administered annually or even semi-annually. As a result, at the insistence of parents, school boards, state legislatures, and national commissions, standardized tests and their results are receiving more attention than at any other time during the last 35 years.

The purpose of this book is to help you and your students get better results on standardized tests. The exercises are grade-specific and based on the most recent versions of these testing instruments:

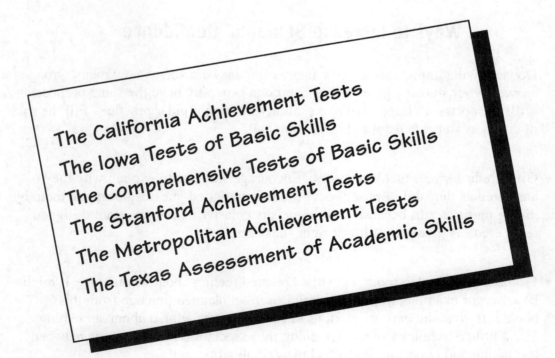

The California Achievement Tests
The Iowa Tests of Basic Skills
The Comprehensive Tests of Basic Skills
The Stanford Achievement Tests
The Metropolitan Achievement Tests
The Texas Assessment of Academic Skills

Exercise materials designed for this book reflect skills from curricula, grade-level tests, and test taking from the California Academic Standards Commission, the New York State Testing Program for Elementary and Intermediate Grades, the Texas Essential Knowledge and Skills program, and the Board of Education for the Commonwealth of Virginia. Your students can expect to meet again on widely used standardized tests most of the content in this book and the style in which questions are posed.

About the Practice Tests

You will notice several things right away about the exercises.

1. The tests are arranged by curricular topics: punctuation, reading comprehension, or adding decimals, for example.

2. The exercises are short enough that you can integrate them into your teaching day. If you spend 20 minutes daily on test taking over several weeks as you approach a test date, your students will build confidence and increase their knowledge base in preparation for the actual test. Becoming familiar with testing formats and practicing on sample questions is one of the most effective ways to improve scores.

3. Examples of student-constructed responses to problems and questions have been included. Students must write, draw, or show their work to get credit for their answers.

Each section of the book—Language Arts, Mathematics, Science, Social Studies—begins with a short lesson for students about answering the questions in that section. A list of test-taking tips appears at the end of the lesson. It would be a good idea to have your students take turns reading portions of the lesson aloud so you can emphasize key suggestions.

Ways to Increase Students' Confidence

- Downplay the importance of how many right answers versus how many wrong answers your students give. These exercises generally have the same purpose as drills in sports—to improve players' ability through regular practice. Fill the role of coach as students learn to hit the long ball.

- Give credit for reasonable answers. Encourage students to explain why they answered as they did. Praise thoughtfulness and good guesses. Surprise them by giving partial credit because their logic is persuasive. On some state-designed tests, credit is given for "almost right" answers.

- Promote in your classroom a positive, relaxed feeling about test taking. It might be wise, for example, to put off administering a planned practice from this booklet if your students are anxious or feeling overwhelmed about something. Use a little psychology in strengthening the association in their minds between test taking and opportunities to feel pleased about oneself.

The following pages provide a list of the basic skills embedded in the tests in this book.

Language Arts

Reading Comprehension
Author's Purpose
Cause and Effect
Compare and Contrast
Conflict
Fact Versus Opinion
Fiction/Nonfiction
Figurative Language
Inferences
Interpreting Graph Sources
Main Ideas
Plot
Poetry and Verse
Point of View
Prediction
Sequencing
Setting
Summary
Supporting Details
Topic Sentences

Research
Dictionary Skills
Encyclopedia
Internet

Vocabulary
Multiple Meanings
Synonym Analogies

Writing
Capitalization
Combining
Editing
Elaborating
Expression
Paragraphing
Punctuation
Sentences
Spelling
Subject-Verb Agreement
Titles
Usage

Mathematics

Averages
Finding Whole Number Averages
Solving Word Problems

Customary Units
Capacity
Length
Measurement
Problem Solving
Temperature
Time
Weight

Decimals
Adding Through Hundredths
Comparing
Place Value
Problem Solving
Rounding
Subtracting Through Hundredths

Division
Problem Solving
Quotients
    Two-Digit
    Three-Digit
    Four-Digit
Solving Word Problems

Estimating

Fractions
Adding Mixed Numerals
Adding with Like Denominators
Adding with Unlike Denominators
Comparing
Equivalents
Simplest Terms
Subtracting Mixed Numerals
Subtracting with Like Denominators
Subtracting with Unlike Denominators

Geometry
Area
Basic Terms
Lines: Segments, Parallel, Intersecting

Mathematics *(cont.)*

Geometry *(cont.)*
Perimeter
Points on a Number Line
Shapes and Angles
Vertices, Edges, and Faces
Volume
Metric Units
Multiplication
Factors
- Two-Digit by One-Digit
- Two-Digit by Two-Digit
- Three-Digit by One-Digit
- Three-Digit by Two-Digit
- Four-Digit by One-Digit
Greatest Common Factor
Least Common Multiple
Multiples of 10, 100, and 1,000
Problem Solving
Solving Word Problems
Multiplication and Division
Patterns
Representing in Picture, Word, and
Number Form
Roman Numerals
Whole Numbers
Adding and Subtracting
Greater and Less Than
Place Value of Whole Numbers
Prime Factorization
Prime Numbers
Rounding
Solving Word Problems

Science

Atmosphere: Weather and Climate
Atoms and Elements
Characteristics of Living Things
Compounds and Chemical Change
Earth Sciences
Ecosystems
Energy and Alternatives
Forms of Energy
Fossils
Fungi
Heat and Matter
Human Body
Magnetism and Electricity
Measuring Work and Force
Mixtures and Solutions
Motion and Force
Plants
Properties of Matter
Protists, Monerans, and Viruses
Scientific Methods
Solar System
Vertebrates and Invertebrates

Social Studies

America's Industrial Revolution
Civil War
Climates
Colonies
Constitution of the United States
Famous Persons
Famous Places
Landforms
Maps and Globes
Native North Americans
Natural Resources
United States: A World Power
Visitors and Explorers in the New World
Westward Movement

Why Take Tests?

The reason is that your teacher, your parents, and school leaders such as the principal all want to know more about what you are learning in school.

They can tell partly from your daily grades, from your reports, and from your work posted on the bulletin board in your classroom, but a test has its own, special purpose. The purpose of a test is to measure what you know and how you think.

There are several ways to do this. A test can be graded by

- how many right answers or how many wrong answers you get.

- how many questions you finish.

- how your score compares to the scores of other students at your school or to scores of other students from all over the United States!

Naturally, you might be asking yourself, "What difference does it make what score I get on a test?" The answer is the scores on tests make a difference to your school and how you are taught.

Here is an example. Imagine that your physical education teacher knows that by October, all fifth graders who are not physically challenged in any special way should be able to run around the school one time without stopping to rest.

She lines everyone up, says, "Ready, set, go!" and everyone starts to run. She writes down the time as each student crosses the finish line. That night, she studies all the finishing times, and she is surprised! The average time it took everyone to finish was longer than what she expected. In fact, a few students had trouble finishing at all, even though they tried their best. Why was the average finishing time longer? Were the students not ready to run that day? Did they not understand the right way to go around the school? Do they need more practice at running long distances? What can the teacher do, she wonders, to improve the students' finishing time?

That is what a test does; it gives teachers, parents, and school administrators clues about what the students can or cannot do and how to help them. Based on test results, a classroom teacher might focus more on teaching fractions, writing, or United States history, for instance. He might try putting students into small reading groups or allowing students to work on math problems in pairs.

As you can see, it is important that you try your best on a test. It makes a big difference between a score that shows what you really know and one that does not represent your ability and understanding.

Turn to the next page to find out how you can "test your best."

Lesson 1: Marking Your Answers

The purpose of this lesson is to introduce you to the correct way to mark your answers on a standardized test.

A standardized test is one that is given to thousands and thousands of students. The writers of the questions try to be as fair as possible. After all, it wouldn't mean anything if all fifth-grade students took different kinds of tests—some easy, some hard. The results would be very confusing and meaningless.

The scoring of standardized tests tries to be as fair as possible, too. It is done by a computer. However, for computer-scored tests, answer sheets must be marked the same way by all students. That is why everyone must use a pencil marked No. 2 and fill in the circles with dark marks.

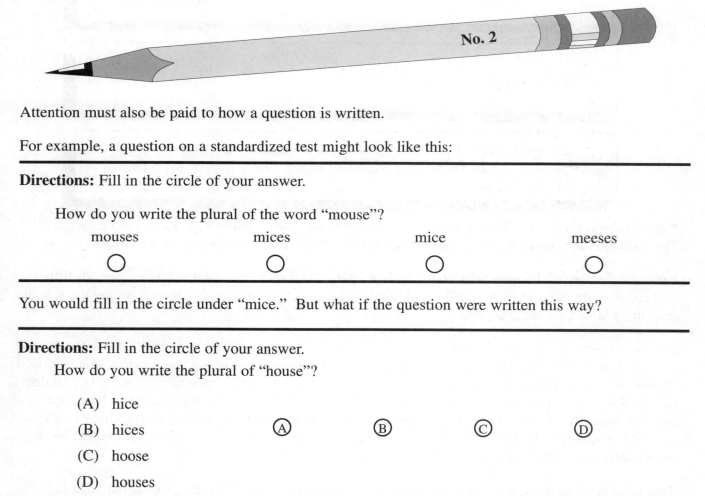

Attention must also be paid to how a question is written.

For example, a question on a standardized test might look like this:

Directions: Fill in the circle of your answer.

How do you write the plural of the word "mouse"?

mouses	mices	mice	meeses
○	○	○	○

You would fill in the circle under "mice." But what if the question were written this way?

Directions: Fill in the circle of your answer.

How do you write the plural of "house"?

(A) hice

(B) hices   Ⓐ   Ⓑ   Ⓒ   Ⓓ

(C) hoose

(D) houses

You would fill in the circle with D inside of it, not fill in the (D) before the word "houses." If you did that, the computer would mark your answer as incorrect. Unfortunately, the computer would have no way of determining that you knew the plural of "house"!

Lesson 1: Marking Your Answers (cont.)

Of course, you will not fill in answers as soon as you are handed a standardized test. The first thing you will do is put your name on the answer sheet. Here is an example:

Each filled-in circle stands for a letter in someone's name. Figure out the person's name by looking at the filled-in circles and then writing the letter of the circle in the empty box above the row. Notice that the person filled in blank circles for spaces anywhere in her name, including leftover spaces at the end. Circles must be filled in under every box.

Did you figure out the person's name?

Last Name   **First Name**

(bubble grid with letters A through Z for each column under Last Name and First Name)

Lesson 2: Minding the Minutes

The purpose of this lesson is to help you learn how to answer the most questions you can on a standardized test.

A standardized test is timed. It is another way of trying to make the test fair. It would not be fair to allow some students to spend an hour solving a dozen one-step math problems—which is much longer than necessary—and a second group of students to spend only fifteen minutes. Would it be clear who understood the problems better? No, it would not be a fair or an accurate measure of the students' abilities.

Keep in mind that you get credit for the number of questions you answer correctly. The more questions you answer correctly, the higher your score. Keeping this in mind, what do you think you should do when you have a limited amount of time to answer a lot of questions?

To answer this question, imagine what you would do in another situation. You are about to play a game outside. In this game, you have ten minutes to gather all the pieces of candy you can. The pieces have been hidden in the grass, in the bushes, and next to stones. Some of them are easy to see; some are well-hidden. Now, what would you do?

You would probably run around and pick up all the pieces you could see right away. If you still had time, you could go back and search for the pieces that are well-hidden. But remember—the idea is to get as many pieces of candy as you can. So go for the easy ones first!

Believe it or not, the same strategy works on a standardized test. See for yourself. Here are three math questions that you must finish with only one minute left on the test.

1.
$$\frac{2}{6}$$
$$+\frac{1}{6}$$
$$\overline{}$$

(A) $\frac{1}{6}$
(B) $\frac{3}{12}$
(C) $\frac{3}{6}$
(D) 3
(E) none of these

Fill in the correct circle.

Ⓐ   Ⓑ   Ⓒ   Ⓓ   Ⓔ

2.
$$\frac{?}{35} = \frac{2}{7}$$

(F) 7
(G) 5
(H) 10
(J) 11
(K) none of these

Fill in the correct circle.

Ⓕ   Ⓖ   Ⓗ   Ⓙ   Ⓚ

3.
$$\frac{3}{8} + \frac{1}{4} =$$

(A) $\frac{2}{4}$
(B) $\frac{2}{8}$
(C) $\frac{4}{12}$
(D) $\frac{4}{8}$
(E) none of these

Fill in the correct circle.

Ⓐ   Ⓑ   Ⓒ   Ⓓ   Ⓔ

Lesson 2: Minding the Minutes (cont.)

You might be able to answer all three problems on the previous page, but if you had to choose, which would you skip? You would probably not try problem 2 since it looks like it would take the longest amount of time to solve.

What if there are 25 math problems on one part of a test and you skipped six of them because they looked like they would take longer to solve? How do you remind yourself to go back? Put a little check mark on your answer sheet next to each problem you skipped. If there is time, you can go back and work on the harder problems.

Here is one more example in which you might have to skip questions on a test, but the choice is a little different. What if there are two reading passages on a test—one has four questions after it, and the other one has eight? You think you only have time to read one of the passages. Which one should you choose?

Choose the one with eight questions after it. Maybe you will only have time to answer six of the eight questions, but you will probably get more of them right than if you read the other passage, answered the four questions, and then were reading the second passage when you ran out of time.

Whenever you can, answer correctly as many questions as you can on a standardized test. That's the smart way to mind the minutes.

Lesson 3: Guessing Correctly

This lesson will explain to you that it is possible to answer a question correctly even if you're just guessing; the secret is narrowing your choices.

Sometimes you will be faced with a really difficult multiple-choice question. It might be that
- you do not understand the question very well.
- you do not understand the answer choices.
- you simply do not know the answer at all.

What should you do? Guess? Yes, you should guess. But you can increase the chance of choosing the correct answer by using a few strategies.

"Best-Guess" Strategies

1. **Always make sure to read all the choices.** Do not jump at the first one that looks like it might be right. Here is an example:

Which is the largest city?

    (A) Los Angeles

    (B) Detroit

    (C) Atlanta

    (D) New York

Fill in the correct circle.

   Ⓐ   Ⓑ   Ⓒ   Ⓓ

Lesson 3: Guessing Correctly *(cont.)*

"Best-Guess" Strategies *(cont.)*

Maybe you do not know which is the largest city, but you do know that (A) "Los Angeles" is bigger than (B) "Detroit," so you choose (A) "Los Angeles" and go on the next question. But wait! It is important to read all the choices. In fact, (D) "New York" is the largest city. You might have guessed between (A) "Los Angeles" or (D) "New York" if you had read all the possible answers. To be a good guesser, you must read every choice—think about each of them, one at a time. If you are the kind of tester who always reads all the choices before choosing one, then you are doing the right thing.

2. Eliminate the answer choices that are plainly wrong.

Here is an example of a social studies question you might find on a test. Choose the correct term.

How can the president stop a law that has been passed by Congress?

    (A) politics

    (B) capital   Fill in the correct circle.

    (C) veto   Ⓐ   Ⓑ   Ⓒ   Ⓓ

    (D) arrest

Think carefully about this situation. Choice (A) "politics" is something like "business" or "teaching"—it is a profession. How could it be used to stop anything? Next, (B) "capital" is usually a place, like a state capital. It could not be used to stop a process like passing a law. What about (D) "arrest"? People do get stopped when they are put "under arrest," but this is a law being talked about, not people, so (D) "arrest" is probably not the correct answer. That leaves (C) "veto" as the most likely choice because each of the other choices does not quite fit for some reason. If you chose (C) "veto," you would be right.

3. Look carefully for clues about how the word is used.

On some tests, you might run across a reading passage that has vocabulary words that you do not know. Here is an example of such a reading passage.

In *The Goats* (1987), Brock Cole's first novel, Howie Mitchell and Laura Golden meet at Tall Pine, a summer camp. They recognize each other as outcasts. "I'm socially retarded for my age," Laura tells Howie. "Yeah. Me too," Howie replies. But deep down, neither of them believes those statements. When a cruel practical joke leaves them abandoned on an island, they seize the opportunity to test their <u>self-reliance</u> and independence. They escape from the island, steer clear of the camp, and make do for themselves. They remain on the run until they are confident they have new identities they can be proud of.

Based on the passage you read, what is the meaning of the word *self-reliance* in this passage?

    (A) personal courage

    (B) tools   Fill in the correct circle.

    (C) meanness   Ⓓ

    (D) depending on oneself

Lesson 3: Guessing Correctly (cont.)

"Best-Guess" Strategies (cont.)

In this case, if you do not know the meaning of the word *self-reliance*, you need to look carefully for clues about how the word is used. The passage says Howie and Laura were abandoned on an island and used the "opportunity to test their self-reliance and courage." Why would they test their (C) "meanness" in such a situation? That does not make much sense. And nothing is said about them having (B) "tools." If they had tools, it would not have been a "cruel practical joke" to leave them abandoned on an island. "Tools" is not a good choice. They might have tested their (A) "personal courage," but the passage also said they "make do for themselves" which suggests (D) "depending on oneself." So both (A) and (D) are likely choices. It is a tossup, but at least you have eliminated two of the four choices, and now you have a fifty-fifty chance of getting the correct answer. Which do you choose, (A) or (D)? The answer is (D) "depending on oneself."

4. **For a math problem, you can use estimating to help you when you are not sure of the answer.**

Now try this problem.

The choir practiced for $2^3/_4$ hours on Saturday and $3^2/_3$ hours on Sunday. How much was the total time?

Fill in the correct circle.

(A) $4^3/_4$
(B) $5^{17}/_{12}$
(C) $5^7/_8$
(D) $6^5/_{12}$

Ⓐ   Ⓑ   Ⓒ   Ⓓ

Maybe this problem gives you trouble because you have difficulty with fractions. Use estimation to help you make your best guess.

Looking at the whole numbers in the problem, the choir practiced 2 hours + 3 hours which totals 5 hours. Five is more than (A) $4^3/_4$ hours. You know that is true even without adding the fractions. (A) cannot be correct. Next, the mixed number (B) $5^{17}/_{12}$ is strange. Have you ever seen a mixed number in which the numerator of the fraction is larger than the denominator? (B) is probably not correct either. (C) $5^7/_8$ is a possibility, but look closely; 8 is not a common denominator of $^3/_4$ and $^2/_3$. How could you get an answer like (C) $5^7/_8$? That leaves (D) $6^5/_{12}$.

If you guessed (D) even without doing the problem, you would be right. You did some quick estimating to solve the problem.

Remember to use these four strategies:

- Make sure to read all the answer choices.
- Eliminate choices that are plainly wrong.
- Look for clues about how a word is used.
- Estimate the answer.

You are sure to raise your test scores if you practice guessing correctly.

Introduction

The language arts section of standardized tests always involves a lot of reading. There are short questions, too, of course, but quite often you must read a paragraph or a long passage to answer the questions.

Here's the Idea

To answer your best on the language arts sections, you must be able to do the following:

1. Identify main ideas.
2. Recognize important details or clues.
3. Draw conclusions on your own.

Before we look at each of the three skills, read the following tips that apply to taking any test, whether it is in language arts, math, science, or social studies. These tips will be repeated because they are important!

Test-Taking Tips

- **Read directions carefully before marking any test questions**, even though you have done that kind of test before. You may think you already know what the directions say, but don't ignore them—read them over. If you do not understand the directions, raise your hand and ask for help. Although your teacher must read the directions exactly as they are written, the teacher can make sure you understand what the directions mean.

- **Follow instructions.** Pay close attention to the sample exercises. They will help you understand what the items on the test will be like and how to mark your answer sheet properly.

- **Read the entire question and all the answer choices.** Do not stop reading when you have found a correct answer. Choices D or E may read "B and D" or "all of the above." On some tests, two answers are both correct. You need to read all the answer choices before marking your answer.

- **For long reading passages, read the questions first so you know what to look for.** If you read the questions first, you will find information in the passage that answers the questions.

- **Remember that taking a test is not a race!** There are no prizes for finishing first. Use all of the time provided for the test. If you have time left over, check your answers.

Try and Discuss

Now let's discuss the same three skills (*identifying main ideas, recognizing important details or clues, and drawing conclusions on your own*) for language arts tests.

Take a look at the question below.

Which one names the whole group?

(A) Earth   Fill in the correct circle.

(B) Mercury

(C) Pluto   (A)   (B)   (C)   (D)   (E)

(D) solar system

(E) orbits

One of these words includes all of the others. It is (D) "solar system." The planets—Earth, Mercury, and Pluto—are all part of the solar system, and all the planets travel in an orbit in the solar system.

The main idea of a paragraph is just like that—it is an idea that names all of the other ideas in the paragraph by making them one group. You will be asked to identify main ideas on language arts tests. You also may be asked, "What would be a good title for this?" which is another way of asking, "What is the main idea?"

This time, look at the list of words below and decide what is the main idea of this group. (**Hint: The main idea is not mentioned!**)

What is the main idea that connects these things?

(A) candles

(B) games

(C) ice cream   What do you think? _____

(D) cake

(E) gifts

(F) guests

Think of a main idea that would include all of these things. You might come to the conclusion that the answer is a *birthday party*. In this case, you have to draw your own conclusion. In other words, you have to make a good guess at what the main idea is, even though it does not appear in words.

Sometimes the main idea of a paragraph is given in words directly—as in the solar system example above—but sometimes the main idea is only suggested, as in the birthday party example.

Try and Discuss *(cont.)*

Now take a look at an actual paragraph. You decide what the main idea is.

Welcome Pool Members!

Welcome to the Millertown pool, created by the parks and recreation department for all residents of Millertown. Please keep in mind that many people use the pool in the summer and that rules must be followed. First, running, pushing, or shoving is never allowed. Walk slowly. Second, do not jump from the side of the pool. You might land on someone and hurt the person. Use the diving board for jumping instead. Third, it is good to have fun in the pool, but no rough play is permitted. If the lifeguard sees dangerous behavior, the swimmers will be told to stop immediately. Enjoy yourself while you're here—Millertown pool is for everyone!

The main idea of this paragraph is

    (A) summer.

    (B) swimming.

    (C) pool safety.

    (D) having fun.

Fill in the correct circle.

Ⓐ   Ⓑ   Ⓒ   Ⓓ

This paragraph is an example of one of those times when you must both recognize important details or clues and draw conclusions on your own.

Eliminate choices by looking for details. For example, you might think that (A) "summer" is correct because, after all, people go to a pool in the summer. But look closely. How many details are about summer in the paragraph? The summer months are not mentioned; the temperature in the summertime is not mentioned. There are no details about summer.

How about choice (B) "swimming"? The paragraph is all about swimming or, at least, using the pool. But in fact, there are no details about how to swim or when to swim. Most of the details—"walk slowly" and "no rough play"—are about safety at the pool. So (C) "pool safety" is the correct answer. What about (D) "having fun"? Draw your own conclusion; see how many details about having fun you can find in the paragraph.

Tips That Help

Remember the following tips:

- The main idea in a paragraph covers all the other ideas in the paragraph or passage.
- Sometimes you must draw your own conclusion. Look for details that support your good guess about what the main idea is.

 Now try the practice tests. Follow the test directions and solve the sample problems to be sure you understand what to do on each test.

Language Arts: Synonym Analogies

An analogy is a way of stating relationships between words or ideas. An analogy may be about synonyms—words that are alike in meaning. An example of this kind of analogy is

well : healthy :: neat : tidy

(well is to healthy as neat is to tidy)

Directions: Complete the synonym analogies, and choose the best answer.

Sample

A. error : mistake :: rash : _____

    (A) careful   (B) careless   (C) eager   (D) wise

---

1. separate : individual :: mixed : _____

    (A) clumsy   (B) picked   (C) mingled   (D) every

---

2. freed : released :: halted : _____

    (F) rewarded   (G) allowed   (H) chose   (J) stopped

---

3. trauma : disturbance :: impact : _____

    (A) siren   (B) brunt   (C) sharpness   (D) emergency

---

4. learning : schooling :: racism : _____

    (F) education   (G) attitude   (H) fairness   (J) bigotry

---

5. contract : agreement :: required : _____

    (A) payment   (B) mandatory   (C) method   (D) business

---

6. believing : faithful :: doubtful : _____

    (F) accepting   (G) tolerance   (H) incredulous   (J) practice

---

7. sad : depressed :: stupor : _____

    (A) night   (B) hunger   (C) friend   (D) daze

---

8. healthy : well :: terminally ill : _____

    (F) sick   (G) recovering   (H) failing   (J) dying

➤ **STOP** ◄

Directions: Read each sentence, and choose the correct way to capitalize the word or group of words that go in the blank. Fill in the answer circle for your choice.

Samples

A. My favorite book is _____.
 (A) *The Trumpeter Swan*
 (B) *the Trumpeter Swan*
 (C) *The trumpeter Swan*
 (D) *the trumpeter swan*

B. *The Wizard of Oz* was written by _____.
 (F) l. Frank Baum
 (G) L. frank Baum
 (H) L. Frank baum
 (J) L. Frank Baum

1. I was in a parade on _____.
 (A) labor day
 (B) Labor day
 (C) Labor Day
 (D) labor Day

5. Have you read the story _____?
 (A) "the Lion and the Mouse"
 (B) "the lion and the mouse"
 (C) "the lion and the Mouse"
 (D) "The Lion and the Mouse"

2. My aunt lives in _____.
 (F) Baltimore, Maryland
 (G) Baltimore, maryland
 (H) baltimore, maryland
 (J) baltimore, Maryland

6. Send the letter to _____.
 (F) mrs. Rose Miller
 (G) Mrs. Rose miller
 (H) mrs. rose miller
 (J) Mrs. Rose Miller

3. The hurricane struck the coast of _____.
 (A) central America
 (B) Central america
 (C) Central America
 (D) central america

7. Chicago is a stop on the _____.
 (A) illinois central Railroad
 (B) Illinois central Railroad
 (C) Illinois Central Railroad
 (D) illinois central railroad

4. We explored a submarine at the _____.
 (F) Museum of science and Industry
 (G) Museum of Science and Industry
 (H) museum of science and Industry
 (J) museum of science and industry

8. Thousands of people visit the _____.
 (F) grand Canyon
 (G) grand canyon
 (H) Grand canyon
 (J) Grand Canyon

➤ STOP ◄

Directions: Read the story below, and choose the best answer for each question.

The Boy Who Drew Cats: A Japanese Fairy Tale

A long time ago, in a little Japanese village, there lived a poor farmer with his wife and family. The eldest son was strong and healthy and helped the farmer in the fields every day, planting and harvesting the rice. The two daughters worked with their mother in the house and the garden. They had been able to work hard from the time they were very little. But the youngest son, although he was extremely clever, was also quite small and frail. He could not work in the rice fields with his father and brother.

One day the boy's parents began to discuss his future, since he was not suited to being a farmer.

His mother said, "Our younger son is very clever. Perhaps we should apprentice him to the priest in the village temple. The priest is getting old, and it may be that our son will make a good priest and will make a suitable helper for the old one." The father agreed that their son's cleverness might make him a suitable candidate for the temple. So the boy's parents went to the village temple to ask the priest to take their son as an acolyte.

When the boy and his parents arrived at the temple, the priest asked the boy several intricate questions. The priest was astonished at the boy's keen understanding and the imaginative answers he gave. Then the old priest agreed to take the boy as an acolyte, with the understanding that the boy would obey him in everything.

The boy tried very hard to obey, and he learned many things, but he had one failing. When he should have been studying his lessons on his own, the boy drew cats instead. He could not help himself for he was an artist at heart. He drew big cats and small cats, fat cats and thin cats, tall cats and short cats, sweet cats and ferocious cats. He drew cats on his lessons, he drew cats on the floor, he drew cats on the walls, and, worst of all, he drew cats on the big, white, rice paper screens in the temple itself.

The old priest was angry at first and told the boy that drawing cats when he should be studying was wrong. But then the priest became sadder and sadder because the boy continued to draw cats when he should have been working on his lessons.

Soon the priest told the boy that he must pack his belongings and go home for an acolyte must obey the priest in all things. The priest said his good-byes and gave the boy one piece of advice.

He said, "Avoid large places at night; keep to small."

Then the priest went into his room and closed the door. The boy did not understand what the priest meant, but he was afraid to knock on the door to ask for an explanation. He packed his few belongings into a bundle and walked down to the main road.

When the little boy reached the road, he thought, "If I go home, my parents will be angry and will punish me. Maybe I should go to the big city and see if the priests in the temple there could use a new apprentice."

He turned away from his home and headed for the city. No one had told the boy that the grand temple in the city had been closed. The boy took his time and enjoyed the walk to the city, looking at the fields and birds and butterflies.

GO →

The Boy Who Drew Cats: A Japanese Fairy Tale (cont.)

It was dark when the boy arrived at the city gates, and everyone was in bed asleep. There was no one to tell him that an evil goblin rat had taken over the temple and chased all the priests and acolytes away. There was no one to tell him that many soldiers had tried to rid the temple of the goblin rat but had failed. Boldly, he walked up to the temple door and knocked on it. Because there was no answer, he knocked several more times. When there still was no answer, he turned the handle and pushed on the door.

It swung wide open, and the boy walked in calling, "Is anyone here?" No one answered him, but he thought that a priest would come by eventually. The boy saw that there was a little room near the door, so he went in and sat down to wait.

Now the goblin always left a light burning in the temple in order to lure strangers in at night. But the little boy had never heard this, so he just waited and inspected the room he was in. It was very dusty and dirty, and he thought that the priests really needed an acolyte to keep it neat and clean. While he was looking around, he opened the drawer in a table and found some rice paper, pens, and ink. Soon he was filling the paper with drawings of cats. When he ran out of paper, he drew cats on the floor. And then he just couldn't help himself. He had to draw cats on the white paper screens in the temple. He drew and drew until they were covered with cats.

When he had filled the screens with pictures of every kind of cat he could imagine, the little boy was very tired. He started to lie down next to one of the screens. But just then the words of the old priest ran through his mind. "Avoid large places; keep to small." The temple was enormous, so the boy looked around for a small place. He found a tiny cupboard in the little room near the door and climbed into it with his parcel of clothes. He shut the cabinet door and was soon fast asleep on a shelf with his bundle for a pillow.

In the middle of the night, the boy heard a loud sound of fighting. It sounded like yowling and running and thumping and bumping and growling. He peeked out of his cubbyhole, but it was too dark. He couldn't see anything, and he was so frightened that he just closed the cabinet door and stayed inside.

In the morning the boy opened the cupboard and crawled out. He tiptoed out of the little room and peeked into the temple. What a surprise! The immense, evil goblin was dead, lying on the temple floor. Who could have killed him? Then the little boy looked at the temple screens. Each cat that he had drawn had a little circle of red around its mouth. And he now understood what the priest meant when he said, "Avoid large places; keep to small."

When the people of the city discovered that the goblin had been defeated, they proclaimed the boy a hero. The soldiers went into the temple to drag the dead goblin away. The priests of that temple would have been happy to take him as an acolyte, but the little boy had changed his mind. He did not become an acolyte or a priest. He became an artist instead, and his paintings of cats were famous in all of Japan. Perhaps the next time you go there, you will see one of his beautiful cats.

GO →

1. Which is the best summary of the story's plot?
   (A) A boy fails to become a priest through laziness.
   (B) A boy discovers he has useful talents after all.
   (C) A goblin rat threatens to destroy temple visitors.
   (D) Long ago, a story became popular in Japan.

2. What is the setting of the story?
   (F) a farm in Japan
   (G) mainly two temples in Japan
   (H) Japan today
   (J) a goblin's cave

3. The point of view of this story is
   (A) the boy's.
   (B) the priest's.
   (C) the boy's parents.
   (D) the author's.

4. How did the priest's advice help the boy?
   (F) He learned to stay away from large cities.
   (G) He learned not to make such big plans for the future.
   (H) He learned to protect himself in strange places.
   (J) He learned to draw small cats, not big ones.

5. What is an "acolyte" in the third paragraph?
   (A) someone who lights candles
   (B) someone who is learning to be a priest
   (C) someone who has no place to go
   (D) someone who is learning to be an artist

6. What killed the giant goblin rat?
   (F) the priest's advice
   (G) the light burning in the temple
   (H) poison on the floor of the temple
   (J) the cats drawn everywhere in the temple

7. The conflict in this fairy tale is
   (A) a boy challenges himself.
   (B) a boy challenges his community.
   (C) a boy challenges nature.
   (D) a boy challenges the supernatural.

8. The author's purpose in this story is to
   (F) warn against not being a good student.
   (G) warn against being different.
   (H) show the power of imagination.
   (J) show how a boy outsmarted everyone.

➤ **STOP** ◄

Language Arts: Poetry and Verse

Directions: Read the two examples of verse and then the poem below. Choose the best answers for the questions.

Crocodilopolis*

In Crocodilopolis
No crocks are afraid,
Their skin is like armor
The color of jade.

Their teeth are so numerous
So jagged and sharp,
That no beast will fight them,
Except for a shark!

With claws set for tearing,
And tails poised to hit,
Their enemies fall dead
Before they get bit!

In Crocodilopolis
The crock has no foe,
But sad is his fate, for
He's friendless, you know!

—Charles J. Shields

* Crocodilopolis was a temple-village in ancient Egypt
where crocodiles were worshipped.

Dark brown is the river,
Golden is the sand.
It flows along forever,
With trees on either hand.
Green leaves a-floating,
Castles of the foam,
Boats of mine a-boating—
When will all come home?
On goes the river,
And out past the mill,
Away down the valley,
Away down the hill.
Away down the river,
A hundred miles or more,
Other little children
Shall bring my boats ashore.

—Robert Louis Stevenson

Pineneedle Street

On Pineneedle Street
No one wants summer to come:
The houses sit deep in snow
All year long.
At both ends of the block—
Where children ride bikes in their shorts,
Or walk home barefoot from the pool
Dripping wet—
They shiver and giggle as they pass Pineneedle Street.
They rub their wet hair with damp towels, laughing,
And wriggle their toes,
Because the icy air sweeping across the snow,
Gives them goose bumps,
Chills their sunburned faces,
And turns their breath to steam.
The firelight shining through the frosted windows,
All along the drifted-in Pineneedle Street,
Warms the families in the houses who stretch, sigh, and say,
"More hot chocolate?
More? Another cold, cozy afternoon in July."
Seated before the fire,
In robes and woolen socks, they watch
Smoke curl up the chimney
Twisting high above the town
Drifting all the way
To the dry, dusty baseball fields
Where it mixes with summer smells of
popcorn, onions, and mustard.
"Hots dogs! Get your hot dogs!"
"But we like it this way," say the families
on Pineneedle Street.
"We do!"
They shovel their walks in the morning,
And touch with their tongues
The tips of icicles hanging over the front door,
To feel the freezing sting.
Then at night,
They carry candles tiredly up to bed,
Scrunch down under the pillows, comforters, and quilts,
And fall asleep, listening to
Snowflakes ticking against the window,
And silver bells ringing merrily
from a white ice-cream truck
passing like a sleigh.

—Charles J. Shields

GO →

1. In "Crocodilopolis," this is an example of a simile:
   (A) No crocks are afraid,
   (B) Their skin is like armor/The color of jade.
   (C) Their teeth are so numerous/So jagged and sharp,
   (D) Before they get bit!

2. What is the point of "Crocodilopolis"?
   (F) Never have anything to do with a crocodile.
   (G) Crocodiles are too powerful.
   (H) Crocodiles will always be alone because they're so fierce.
   (J) No one understands crocodiles very well.

3. Which statement is true about "Crocodilopolis"?
   (A) The author used rhyme.
   (B) All lines have the same number of syllables.
   (C) Crocodiles travel alone.
   (D) The verse is not supposed to be humorous.

4. What is an example of imagery in "Pineneedle Street"?
   (F) Where children ride bikes in their shorts,
   (G) Because the icy air sweeping across the snow,/Gives them goose bumps,
   (H) "But we like it this way," say the families
   (J) On Pineneedle Street/No one wants summer to come:

5. "Pineneedle Street" is about
   (A) a lonely town.
   (B) how winter stays too long.
   (C) why people prefer summer to winter.
   (D) some people's stubbornness.

6. What is the correct order that things happen in the poem by Robert Louis Stevenson?
   1—The boats float past the mill.
   2—Children find the boats.
   3—The writer puts his boats in the river.
   4—The boats float a hundred miles.
   (F) 2-1-3-4
   (G) 3-4-1-2
   (H) 3-1-4-2
   (J) 4-1-2-3

7. Write three words that could describe the boats' trip down the river.

8. The poet asks, "Boats of mine a-boating/When will all come home?" Will the boats come home? Explain.

9. What is the setting of the poem by Robert Louis Stevenson?
   (A) the ocean
   (B) a forest
   (C) a river
   (D) a waterfall

10. Write a title for the poem:

➤ **STOP** ◄

Directions: Read the sentences below. Choose the sentence that is punctuated correctly. Mark the choice "none of these" if none of the sentences is correct.

Sample

A. Which sentence is punctuated correctly?
 (A) "Why does the local news begin at six oclock?" Debra asked.
 (B) "Why does the local news begin at six o'clock," Debra asked.
 (C) Why does the local news begin at six oclock?" Debra asked.
 (D) "Why does the local news begin at six o'clock?" Debra asked.
 (E) none of these

---

1. Which sentence is punctuated correctly?
 (A) Carlos leaned out of the window and yelled Hey! Wait up!"
 (B) Carlos leaned out of the window and yelled, "Hey! Wait up"
 (C) Carlos leaned out of the window and yelled, Hey! Wait up!
 (D) Carlos leaned out of the window and yelled, "Hey! Wait up!"
 (E) none of these

2. Which sentence is punctuated correctly?
 (F) The lady in the office is named Ms, Holly.
 (G) The lady in the office, is named Ms. Holly.
 (H) The lady in the office is named Ms Holly.
 (J) The lady in the office is named Ms. Holly.
 (K) none of these

3. Which is punctuated correctly?
 (A) It's warm today Do you want to play outside?
 (B) Its warm today, Do you want to play outside.
 (C) Its warm today. Do you want to play outside.
 (D) It's warm today. Do you want to play outside?
 (E) none of these

4. Which sentence is punctuated correctly?
 (F) Meet me at ten oclock, all right?
 (G) Meet me at ten o'clock, all right.
 (H) Meet me at ten o'clock, all right?
 (J) Meet me at ten oclock all right.
 (K) none of these

5. Which sentence is punctuated correctly?
 (A) Mrs. Washington the principal, says the play starts at 2 P.M.
 (B) Mrs Washington, the principal, says the play starts at 2 P.M.
 (C) Mrs. Washington the principal says the play starts at 2 P.M.
 (D) Mrs. Washington, the principal, says the play starts at 2 P.M.
 (E) none of these

6. Which sentence is punctuated correctly?
 (F) The list of party supplies included; cake, candles, and three gallons of ice cream.
 (G) The list of party supplies included, cake, candles, and three gallons of ice cream.
 (H) The list of party supplies included cake candles, and three gallons of ice cream.
 (J) The list of party supplies included cake, candles, and three gallons of ice cream.
 (K) none of these

 ➤ STOP ◄

Directions: Read questions 1–12, and fill in the correct circle.

1. You are writing a report on former President Richard Milhous Nixon. In which volume of the encyclopedia would you look?
   (A) Ru-Sap
   (B) Min-Pam
   (C) Ma-Mil
   (D) Pan-Ro

2. Now you have to look up the location and characteristics of the Sahara Desert in northern Africa. Which volume would you choose?
   (F) Ru-Sap
   (G) Pan-Ro
   (H) Min-Pam
   (J) none of these

3. Finally, you need to look up information about the Mississippi River for social studies. Which volume would you choose?
   (A) Pan-Ro
   (B) Min-Pam
   (C) Ru-Sap
   (D) Go-Ja

4. When reading your math textbook, you are not sure of the definition of "quotient." Where would you look in your textbook for a definition?
   (F) index
   (G) table of contents
   (H) appendix
   (J) glossary

5. You need three words that have the same meaning as "slow." Where would you look?
   (A) a dictionary
   (B) a thesaurus
   (C) an encyclopedia
   (D) an atlas

6. Look at the Web site addresses below. At which one would you expect to find information about national parks?
   (F) www.campnet.com
   (G) www.outdoors.org
   (H) www.dep.interior.gov
   (J) www.indiana.edu

7. Which would be a topic you could research for a science fair project?
   (A) animals
   (B) Does water always boil at 212 degrees Fahrenheit?
   (C) How big is the universe?
   (D) my favorite game

Directions: For the following questions, choose A if the title sounds like fiction or B if it sounds like nonfiction.

8. *Fish in Rivers and Streams*
   (A) fiction   (B) nonfiction

9. *Video Games of 1999*
   (A) fiction   (B) nonfiction

10. *My Teacher Is a Martian!*
    (A) fiction   (B) nonfiction

11. *Famous Women Inventors*
    (A) fiction   (B) nonfiction

12. *The Ghost of the Dreadmire*
    (A) fiction   (B) nonfiction

GO →

Directions: Sometimes you must look up information about a book or an author for a report. Read the book review below. Choose the best answer for each question.

This Saga Sags

Review: *The Transall Saga* by Gary Paulsen. Delacorte Press, 1998. 248 pages. $15.95.

A tube of bluish-white light projecting skyward from a fallen fireball fascinates thirteen-year-old Mark Harrison, camped alone on a canyon floor in Gary Paulsen's most recent novel for young people, *The Transall Saga*. Mark, in the middle of a week-long survival trek across the desert, approaches the light, accidentally tumbles into its beam, and is instantly transported to a bleak, rust-colored world of howling creatures and quicksand.

The author, however, is on familiar ground. Having written exciting stories in lean, sure-footed prose about the trials of Brian Robeson in *Hatchet* and Russel Suskitt in *Dogsong*, both of whom find self-understanding in the wilderness, Paulsen once again places an adolescent boy in an unforgiving landscape and expects him to get moving.

Unfortunately, Mark never really does get moving. For some reason, Paulsen stacks the deck in his favor by telling us, "Hiking and backpacking were Mark's one obsession." Consequently, Mark does pretty well on his own: "Life was simple. Find food, scout the countryside, try to make new things, and sleep." Sounds easy enough, doesn't it?

Second, the author casts away the heart of all good young adult novels: Mark doesn't change—not a whit. Unlike Brian in *Hatchet*, who learned from his mistakes and built his virtues slowly on a foundation of sheer determination, Mark, after four years spent in the fierce world called Transall, seems to be the same—except that at 17 he looks like Conan the Barbarian.

In fact, the novel presses so heavily on the pedal of male fantasy-adventure that characterization gets left in the dust. Girls in particular don't come off well. Mark, called Krakon by the people of Transall, is advised, "It is a dangerous thing to have women sew for you, Krakon. Next thing you know, they will be telling you to take a bath." Har-har!

The Transall Saga deposits Mark back in his own time after an absence of four years, but no one seems to care. Readers may not, either. A clue as to why may be because Paulsen published eight young-adult novels in 1995 alone. Perhaps it's not how long Mark spent in Transall but how long the author spent putting him there.

— Charles J. Shields

13. Who is the author of the book?
(A) Charles J. Shields
(B) Mark Harrison
(C) Gary Paulsen
(D) Delacorte Press

14. What is a summary of the plot of the book?
(F) A young man is lost with only a hatchet to help him.
(G) A young man meets up with Conan the Barbarian.
(H) A young man is mysteriously transported to a different world.
(J) A young man resists being taken care of by women.

15. Which of the following is true?
(A) The author has written other books like *The Transall Saga*.
(B) The author worked for several years on the book.
(C) This is the author's first book.
(D) The character, Mark Harrison, changes a lot in the book.

16. What is the writer's opinion of *The Transall Saga*?
(F) Not very much happens in the book.
(G) It's one of the author's best.
(H) The title of the book is unclear.
(J) The author continues to be one of the best writers around.

 **STOP**

Directions: Answer the questions in italics.

Sample

A. Combine these sentences. "One-third of Earth's surface is desert. It is land with little rainfall." *Which sounds best?*

(A) Little rain falls on the desert.

(B) One-third of Earth's surface is desert, where there is little rainfall.

(C) One-third of the desert gets little rainfall.

(D) Receiving little rainfall, the desert covers one-third of Earth's surface.

---

1. Combine these sentences: "Deserts are always dry. They may be hot. They may be cold." *Which sounds best?*

   (A) Hot and cold, deserts are dry.

   (B) Deserts are always dry, but they may be hot or cold.

   (C) Hot deserts or cold deserts, but they are always dry.

   (D) They are always dry. Deserts are hot or cold.

---

2. Combine these sentences: "Deserts make good laboratories. Scientists can study well-preserved fossils there. It's because deserts are so dry." *Which sounds best?*

   (F) Dry deserts make good laboratories for studying well-preserved fossils.

   (G) Well-preserved fossils are in deserts, which are so dry; scientists can study them.

   (H) Because deserts are so dry, they make good laboratories for scientists studying well-preserved fossils.

   (J) Why do scientists study fossils in the desert? It's because they are so dry.

---

3. "Very little vegetation lives in the desert." *What is the subject of the sentence?*

   (A) desert

   (B) vegetation

   (C) very little

   (D) lives

---

4. "Deserts can be easily damaged even though they are harsh environments." *What is subject of the sentence?*

   (F) they

   (G) environments

   (H) deserts

   (J) damaged

> **STOP**

Directions: Read the sentence carefully. Fill in the circle for any word that is misspelled. If all the words are correct, fill in the circle for "no mistake."

Samples

A. The <u>sled</u> <u>bounced</u> down the hill to the edge of the <u>streem</u>. <u>no mistake</u>
       A   B   C   D

B. The <u>bus</u> <u>stopped</u> in front of the train <u>station</u>. <u>no mistake</u>
       F   G   H   J

---

1. His <u>birthday</u> party is <u>planed</u> for <u>Wednesday</u>. <u>no mistake</u>
         A   B   C   D

---

2. No one <u>new</u> who <u>shouted</u>, "<u>Batter</u> up!" <u>no mistake</u>
        F   G   H   J

---

3. The mother <u>hid</u> the <u>kittens</u> under the <u>stares</u>. <u>no mistake</u>
         A   B   C   D

---

4. He <u>appeared</u> <u>before</u> the <u>committee</u>, acting nervous. <u>no mistake</u>
       F   G   H   J

---

5. Please <u>procede</u> to the ticket <u>window</u> <u>straight</u> ahead. <u>no mistake</u>
        A   B   C   D

---

6. Did you <u>believe</u> the <u>storey</u> about the <u>queen</u>? <u>no mistake</u>
       F   G   H   J

---

7. The <u>thieves</u> left <u>there</u> fingerprints on the <u>money</u>. <u>no mistake</u>
        A   B   C   D

---

8. The <u>general</u> gave a <u>comand</u>, and the soldiers <u>obeyed</u>. <u>no mistake</u>
       F   G   H   J

---

9. The police <u>officer</u> directs <u>traffick</u> every day near the <u>bakery</u>. <u>no mistake</u>
       A   B   C   D

---

10. Snow on the <u>mountain</u> melted, <u>filling</u> the lake in the <u>valley</u> below. <u>no mistake</u>
       F   G   H   J

➤ STOP ◄

Directions: Read the paragraph or sentence. Choose the best topic sentence for the paragraph.

Sample

A. _____ Many kinds of mammals hibernate. They hibernate for two reasons. First, there is usually not much food for them in winter. Second, the cold winter weather is hard to stand. During hibernation, a mammal remains very still, and its heart rate slows down. Its body needs less energy. Needing less energy, the sleeping animal is able to survive on its own stored fat without searching for food very often.

(A) Animals can be found everywhere.
(B) Hibernation helps animals that live in cold climates to survive.
(C) Sleeping beneath the ground is not something people do.
(D) Have you ever seen an animal in the snow?

---

1. _____ Marking dangerous waters, lighthouses played a vital role in guiding ships safely into port. Trade would have suffered without them. Sixteen lighthouses were already in place when the American colonies formed the United States. Building lighthouses was one of the new government's first goals. Hundreds more lighthouses were built later along our seacoasts and on the Great Lakes, creating the world's largest aids to a navigation system. No other national lighthouse system compares with that of the United States in number and variety of lighthouses.

(A) Never go sailing unless you know exactly where you are.
(B) Many lighthouses have been turned into museums.
(C) Lighthouses are reminders of the United States' history.
(D) Some lighthouses include rooms for the lighthouse keeper and his family.

---

2. _____ According to legend, Edgar Allan Poe was in a tavern in October, 1849. He staggered out into the street and fell down. He was taken to a hospital, but by the next day he was sweating heavily and shouting at invisible people. He acted confused and angry for several days. On the fourth day, he quieted down and died. Since then, most of Poe's biographers said he died abusing alcohol, but Dr. R. Michael Benitz presented another opinion in an article in a medical journal after studying the record of Poe's death. Dr. Benitz wrote that Poe died of rabies, not alcohol abuse. Rabies from the bite of a diseased animal would explain the writer's strange behavior, especially his rage and confusion.

(F) It's hard to know what to think sometimes about what happened in the past.
(G) A doctor may have found the truth about the mysterious death of Edgar Allan Poe, the writer of famous horror stories.
(H) Edgar Allan Poe wrote horror stories that still appear in school textbooks.
(J) We will probably never know the whole truth about what happened to Edgar Allan Poe.

---

3. _____ There is a poisonous gas that kills nearly 300 people in their homes each year. It has no odor. What's more, it has no taste and no color. It is very dangerous. Carbon monoxide is a gas that comes from burning any fuel. Anything in your home that burns fuel, such as a gas oven or furnace, can give off carbon monoxide gas. But when things that burn fuel are kept in good order, they don't give off carbon monoxide. The best way to prevent carbon monoxide poisoning is to keep gas ovens, furnaces, and fireplaces clean and repaired.

(A) Have you practiced fire safety in your home?
(B) This gas is carbon monoxide.
(C) Have you heard about the invisible killer?
(D) It is not the same as carbon dioxide.

➤ **STOP** ◄

Directions: Look for a usage mistake in each item. Fill in the answer circle for the number of the line with the mistake. If you do not find a mistake, fill in the answer circle with "no mistake."

Samples

A. (A) Tim went to the corner

   (B) to wait for the bus. He waves

   (C) as it approached.

   (D) no mistake

B. (F) The river runs south for

   (G) hundreds of miles before

   (H) reaching the sea.

   (J) no mistake

1. (A) Lupe opened the door of

   (B) the refrigerator hopefully,

   (C) but there were nothing inside.

   (D) no mistake

2. (F) It took Robert three hours

   (G) to rake them leaves up.

   (H) He finished at noon.

   (J) no mistake

3. (A) My mother gave us five

   (B) dollars for the carnival.

   (C) Me and Manny thanked her.

   (D) no mistake

4. (F) Kent found a field mouse

   (G) in his backyard. He brung

   (H) a drawing of it to school.

   (J) no mistake

5. (A) My sister hasn't never

   (B) gone to bed without saying

   (C) good night to all of us.

   (D) no mistake

6. (F) The coach talked

   (G) to Sheila and her

   (H) about the playoffs.

   (J) no mistake

7. (A) My sister Tasha she has

   (B) a game that's missing the

   (C) directions, so we pretend.

   (D) no mistake

8. (F) Why you always telling

   (G) Mrs. Mikes about the

   (H) game we lost?

   (J) no mistake

9. (A) Mom wasn't feeling well.

   (B) Dad said him and me

   (C) would go shopping ourselves.

   (D) no mistake

10. (F) My brother isn't in school

   (G) yet. He ask a lot of questions

   (H) about what it's like.

   (J) no mistake

➤ STOP ◄

Directions: Read the sentences below, and answer the question.

Imagine this situation. Many new homes are being built near your school. Soon, several hundred new students will be arriving at your school. The principal has an idea. She says that to prevent overcrowding, the school day should be divided in half. One-half of the students will attend from 7 A.M. until noon. The other half will attend from 12 P.M. until 5 P.M. What do you think are the advantages and disadvantages of this idea?

Write a paragraph explaining your reasons.

_____

_____

_____

_____

_____

_____

_____

_____

_____

Teacher Note: Student responses are to be evaluated by the teacher.

➤ **STOP** ◄

Introduction

To perform your best on the mathematics section of a standardized test, you need not know the right answer every time. But you do need to use two important strategies that will improve your score: *estimating* and *recognizing a reasonable answer*.

Here's the Idea

Estimating is a way of getting close to a right answer by rounding. When you round numbers in a problem, you will get an answer that is close to the right answer.

Recognizing a reasonable answer means deciding that an answer choice is probably right, based on what you already know about numbers and problems. You can drop some answer choices right away because they are not reasonable.

However, before we look at these two skills, below are some tips that apply to taking any test, whether it's in language arts, math, science, or social studies. These tips will be repeated because they're important!

Test-Taking Tips

- **Read directions carefully before marking any test questions,** even though you have done that kind of test before. You may think you already know what the directions say, but don't ignore them—read them over. If you don't understand the directions, raise your hand and ask for help. Although your teacher must read the directions exactly as they are written, the teacher can make sure you understand what the directions mean.

- **Follow instructions.** Pay close attention to the sample exercises. They will help you understand what the items on the test will be like and how to mark your answer sheet properly.

- **Read the entire question and all the answer choices.** Do not stop reading when you have found a correct answer. Choices D or E may read "B and D" or "all of the above." On some tests, two answers are both correct. You need to read all the answer choices before marking your answer.

- **And remember—taking a test is not a race!** There are no prizes for finishing first. Use all of the time provided for the test. If you have time left over, check your answers.

Try and Discuss

Now let's discuss those two skills for mathematics tests—*estimating* and *recognizing a reasonable answer*. When you estimate, you use round numbers to come close to the correct answer without even working the problem through. Use these two rules for rounding:

- Round <u>up</u> for numbers five or greater than five.
- Round <u>down</u> for numbers less than five.

For example, round the numbers in this problem to find the answer—do not work the problem on paper! Just round the numbers in your mind.

$23 + 16 =$	(A) 7 (B) 29 (C) 39 (D) 216	Fill in the correct circle. (A)　(B)　(C)　(D)

Remember the rules of rounding. Round down 23 to 20 because 3 is less than 5. Then round up 16 to 20 because 6 is greater than 5. That makes the problem in your mind 20 + 20 = (?). The answer to that problem is 40. Which answer choice is closest to 40? You can use estimating for very large problems, too. Try this one:

2,379 + 4,675	(A) 7,054 (B) 8,987 (C) 3,465 (D) 2,004	Fill in the correct circle. (A)　(B)　(C)　(D)

Round down 2,379 to 2,000. Then round up 4,675 to 5,000. You can add 2,000 + 5,000 in your head. It's 7,000. Which answer comes closest? Estimating works well when you do not know the answer or you are trying to go faster on a test because time is short. Now what about recognizing a reasonable answer? Reasonable means "likely based on careful thinking." For instance, when you see the following problem, you know that 8,000 is clearly not a reasonable answer.

20 x 4	(A) 8,000 (B) 60 (C) 80 (D) 20	Fill in the correct circle. (A)　(B)　(C)　(D)

Think it through: four 20s would never total 8,000! Also, multiplying 20 by 4 could not result in 20 again—that is not a reasonable answer either. You know these things already. Recognizing a reasonable answer is a powerful strategy when you want to eliminate answers. In other words, you can drop some answer choices immediately because they are not reasonable. Don't bother with answer choices that are clearly wrong because they are unreasonable. This improves your chances of choosing the correct answer even if you have difficulty doing the problem.

Tips That Help

Remember the following:

- Use estimating to come close to the correct answer.
- Learn to recognize a reasonable answer so you can eliminate choices that are clearly wrong.

 Now try the practice tests, listening to your teacher's directions.

Directions: Fill in the circle for the correct answer to each problem about finding averages.

Sample

A. Find the average of 17, 21, and 58.

    (A) 30   (B) 32   (C) 6.66   (D) 31

1. Find the average of 14, 22, and 297.

    (A) 111.3   (B) 110   (C) 111   (D) 87

2. Find the average of 26, 22, and 99.

    (F) 48.6   (G) 49.3   (H) 17   (J) 49

3. Andrew bowled two games, scoring 193 and 206. What must he bowl in the third game in order to average 200 for the 3 games?

    (A) 196   (B) 201   (C) 199   (D) It's not possible.

4. Use the table below. It shows the number of books read by a group of fifth-grade students during the second semester.

Name	Books Read
Holly	6
Tiffany	4
Lauren	7
Kristin	3
Kyle	5
Heidi	5
Andrew	8
Dustin	2

What is the average number of books read by students in this group?

    (F) 6   (G) 5   (H) 7   (J) 8

5. What is the average for the three students who read the most?

    (A) 6   (B) 21   (C) 3   (D) 7

6. So far in math class, your scores on tests have been 98, 92, 80, and 90. Your average is

    (F) 94   (G) 93   (H) 85   (J) 90

➤ **STOP** ◄

Mathematics: Customary and Metric Units

Directions: Read the questions, and circle the correct answers.

Trains to University Park

Name	Leaves	Arrives
Flyer	5:02 P.M.	5:40 P.M.
Red Line	5:30 P.M.	6:10 P.M.
Sunset	5:45 P.M. *(makes one stop)*	6:30 P.M.

1. How long does the Flyer take to get to University Park?

   (A) 38 minutes   (C) 42 minutes

   (B) 1 hour, 2 minutes   (D) 36 minutes

2. How long does the Red Line take to get to University Park?

   (F) 40 minutes   (H) 50 minutes

   (G) 20 minutes   (J) 1 hour, 10 minutes

3. If the Sunset goes as fast as the Red Line train, how much time does the extra stop take?

   (A) 5 minutes   (C) 1 hour, 15 minutes

   (B) 10 minutes   (D) 15 minutes

4. How long is this pencil?

   (F) 4 1/2 inches

   (G) 3 3/4 inches

   (H) 4 1/4 inches

   (J) .23 inches

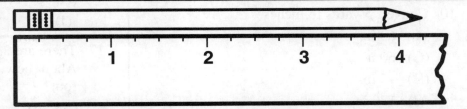

5. How many degrees difference is there between thermometers A and B?

   (A) 24 degrees

   (B) 26 degrees

   (C) 8 degrees

   (D) 40 degrees

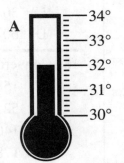
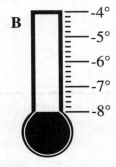

6. A spaghetti recipe calls for one pound of stewed tomatoes. Robby has a can of stewed tomatoes in the cupboard that says "32 oz." How many pounds is in the can in the cupboard?

   (F) 4   (H) 1

   (G) 2   (J) 3

GO →

7. What is the Roman numeral for 29?
   (A) XXXI
   (B) XXXVIV
   (C) XXVIIII
   (D) XVVIIII

8. Ron wants to make a special kind of punch that needs 1/2 gallon of ginger ale. He has a quart of ginger ale in the refrigerator. How much more does he need?
   (F) 3 quarts
   (G) 2 quarts
   (H) 1 quart
   (J) 2 cups

9. A package of cookies says there are two dozen inside. How many are in there?
   (A) 20
   (B) 22
   (C) 12
   (D) 24

10. Convert 5 yards to inches.
    (F) 63 in.
    (G) 60 in.
    (H) 15 in.
    (J) 180 in.

11. Convert 15 inches to feet.
    (A) 5 ft.
    (B) 180 ft.
    (C) 45 ft.
    (D) 1 1/4 ft.

12. About how tall is a regular door?
    (F) 72 inches
    (G) 7 feet
    (H) 12 feet
    (J) 12 inches

13. Two meters is how many centimeters?
    (A) 20   (C) 2000
    (B) 200   (D) 20,000

14. A kilogram is 1,000 grams. Marc picked 3 kilograms of blueberries at a farm in Michigan. His mom used 2,000 grams for muffins. How many kilograms of blueberries are left over?
    (F) 2
    (G) 1/2
    (H) 1
    (J) 5

15. Grandpa Morgan's deck behind his house is 18 feet wide. How many yards wide is it?
    (A) 6
    (B) 3
    (C) 15
    (D) 9

16. A quart of milk is half empty. How many cups are left?
    (F) 2
    (G) 4
    (H) 6
    (J) 1

17. There are 2.54 centimeters in an inch. About how many centimeters are there in 1 foot?
    (A) 10
    (B) 20
    (C) 30
    (D) 60

18. Convert 14 feet, 10 inches to inches.
    (F) 158 inches
    (G) 52 inches
    (H) 140 inches
    (J) 178 inches

➤ STOP ◄

Directions: Fill in the circle for the correct answer to each division problem.

Sample

A. $665 \div 7 =$

    (A) 93   (B) 92 r 6   (C) 95   (D) 96

---

1. The same number of cheerleaders stood in each line. There were four lines. There were 16 cheerleaders. How many cheerleaders were in each line?

    (A) 2   (B) 12   (C) 4   (D) 6

---

2. $3{,}996 \div 27 =$

    (F) 138   (G) 148   (H) 146   (J) 144

---

3. $380 \div 20 =$

    (A) 19.47   (B) 1,948   (C) 194   (D) 19

---

4. $1{,}748 \div 23 =$

    (F) 76   (G) 66   (H) 7.6   (J) 6.6

---

5. Juan typed 45 math problems in 9 minutes. How many problems did he type in one minute?

    (A) 5 problems (B) 6 problems (C) 54 problems (D) 14 problems

---

6. $224 \div 4 =$

    (F) 58   (G) 56   (H) 5.8   (J) 77

---

7. Write the quotient for $38 \div 8$ in remainder form.

    (A) 4 6/8   (B) 4.6   (C) 4 r 6   (D) 4 4/6

---

8. $1{,}235 \div 19 =$

    (F) 650   (G) 55   (H) 65   (J) 6.5

GO →

9. $165 \div 11 =$

    (A) 15   (B) 13   (C) 150   (D) 1.5

10. $3{,}597 \div 33 =$

    (F) 99   (G) 109   (H) 99   (J) 19

11. Mr. Anders is a salesman. He drives 140 miles Monday through Friday. How many miles does he drive each day?

    (A) 20   (B) 28   (C) 26   (D) 24

12. $630 \div 9 =$

    (F) 7   (G) 70   (H) 700   (J) 807

13. $1{,}350 \div 25 =$

    (A) 54   (B) 56   (C) 64   (D) 66

14. Coach Smith is adding grandstands to the football field. He needs to seat 1,500 people. Each grandstand seats a maximum of 500. How many should he order?

    (F) 10   (G) 30   (H) 3   (J) 5

15. $200 \div [?] = 4$

    (A) 80   (B) 800   (C) 50   (D) 500

16. Marc has 140 cards in his collection. Half of them are sports figures. Half of that number are musicians. How many are musicians?

    (F) 70   (G) 45   (H) 35   (J) 30

17. $350 \div 10 =$

    (A) 3,500   (B) 35   (C) 35.1   (D) 450

18. $432 \div 12 =$

    (F) 40 r 2   (G) 306   (H) 362   (J) 36

➤ **STOP** ◄

Mathematics: Fractions—Equivalents and Simplest Terms

Directions: Fill in the circle for the correct answer to each problem.

Samples

A. Which is another way of expressing 28/21?

    (A) 4/3   (B) 9   (C) 3/4   (D) 27

B. Write the ratio 4 to 74 as a fraction in simplest form.

    (F) 2/37   (G) 74/4   (H) 4.74   (J) 4:74

1. Which two fractions are equivalent to 5/9?

    (A) 10/27, 15/18   (B) 10/18, 25/81   (C) 10/18, 15/27   (D) 25/81, 15/27

2. What is the ratio of stars (*) to number signs (#)?

    ##*##*##*##*##

    (F) 4:5   (G) 5:9   (H) 9:5   (J) 4:9

3. Which three fractions are equivalent to 1/3?

    (A) 3/12, 4/12, 3/9   (B) 4/12, 2/6, 3/9   (C) 2/6, 3/9, 9/12   (D) 3/12, 3/6, 3/9

4. In a sack of bird seed, the ratio of sunflower seeds to corn kernels is 250 to 1000. Write this ratio as a fraction in its simplest form.

    (F) 1/4   (G) 1/8   (H) 250/1000   (J) 1/2

5. Write 18/21 in its simplest form.

    (A) 7/6   (B) 6/7   (C) 3   (D) 18

6. Write 80/90 in its simplest form.

    (F) 80   (G) 8/9   (H) 9/8   (J) 10

7. Write 10/12 in its simplest form.

    (A) 6/5   (B) 2   (C) 5/6   (D) 10

GO →

8. Find the ratio of the rectangle's width to its length in the simplest form.

5 cm

8 cm

   (F) 3/8   (G) 5/8   (H) 3/5   (J) 1/2

Solve the proportions.

9. 30/45 = 2/?

   (A) 5   (B) 15   (C) 10   (D) 3

10. 4/9 = ?/27

   (F) 12   (G) 24   (H) 29   (J) 8

11. Write 41/6 as a mixed number.

   (A) 6 5/6   (B) 41 1/6   (C) 7 5/6   (D) 1 35/6

12. Charlie sold 36 tickets to the Thanksgiving Day dinner for his club. Dustin sold 30. What is the ratio of the number of tickets Charlie sold to the number of tickets Dustin sold?

   (F) 5/6   (G) 6/5   (H) 11/5   (J) 5/11

13. Which group of fractions is equivalent to 1/10?

   (A) 1/100, 3/30   (B) 2/20, 1/100   (C) 2/30, 3/20   (D) 2/20, 3/30

14. Find the common denominator of 3/6 and 2/7.

   (F) 7   (G) 3   (H) 13   (J) 42

15. Find the least common denominator of 5/7 and 5/56.

   (A) 224   (B) 56   (C) 28   (D) 112

16. Find the least common denominator of 3/4 and 1/2.

   (F) 2   (G) 1   (H) 4   (J) 3

➤ **STOP** ◄

Directions: Fill in the circle for the correct answer to each problem.

Samples

A. Use prime factorization to find the least common multiple of 40 and 48.

    (A) 120   (B) 240   (C) 960   (D) 8

B. Find the smallest number whose factors include 3, 11, and 5.

    (F) 33   (G) 26   (H) 19   (J) 165

---

1. Use prime factorization to find the least common multiple of 72 and 24.

    (A) 24   (B) 216   (C) 72   (D) 36

---

2. Find the smallest number whose factors include 7, 2, and 4.

    (F) 13   (G) 14   (H) 28   (J) 30

---

3. Find the smallest number whose factors include 11, 7, and 121.

    (A) 847   (B) 139   (C) 77   (D) 1,338

---

4. Find the greatest common factor of 24 and 2.

    (F) 1   (G) 4   (H) 3   (J) 2

---

5. For Halloween, Spencer got 18 candy bars, 12 gumballs, and 36 chocolate drops. He wants to divide it all into groups so that each group has an equal number of candy bars, an equal number of gumballs, and an equal number of chocolate drops. What is the maximum number of groups he can make?

    (A) 2   (B) 6   (C) 12   (D) 3

---

6. Find the greatest common factor of 36 and 6.

    (F) 3   (G) 6   (H) 12   (J) 9

GO →

Mathematics: Factorization *(cont.)*

7. Mrs. Mikes, who runs the James Hart School store, has 28 tablets of paper, 98 erasers, and 196 pencils. She wants to divide the supplies into groups so that each group has an equal number of tablets, an equal number of erasers, and an equal number of pencils. What is the maximum number of groups she can make?

    (A) 7   (B) 2   (C) 28   (D) 14

8. Find the smallest number whose factors include 2, 11, and 121.

    (F) 22   (G) 253   (H) 242   (J) 134

9. Use prime factorization to find the least common multiple of 48 and 24.

    (A) 24   (B) 96   (C) 48   (D) 16

10. Eli is trying to organize his toolbox. He has 50 bolts, 20 nuts, and 100 washers. He wants to divide it all into groups so that each group has an equal number of bolts, an equal number of nuts, and an equal number of washers. What is the maximum number of groups he can make?

    (F) 2   (G) 10   (H) 5   (J) 20

11. Use prime factorization to find the least common multiple of 75 and 45.

    (A) 75   (B) 225   (C) 1,125   (D) 15

12. Find the greatest common factor of 36 and 54.

    (F) 18   (G) 9   (H) 3   (J) 6

13. Use prime factorization to find the least common multiple of 90 and 72.

    (A) 360   (B) 2,160   (C) 120   (D) 18

14. Find the smallest number whose factors include 7, 2, and 49.

    (F) 345   (G) 14   (H) 58   (J) 98

➤ **STOP** ◄

Mathematics: Fractions—Adding and Subtracting

Directions: Fill in the circle for the correct answer to each problem.

Samples

A. 5/6 - 1/3 =

    (A) 2/9   (B) 5/18   (C) 7/6   (D) 1/2

B. 4/5 + 1/10 =

    (F) 9/10   (G) 1   (H) 1 1/10   (J) 8/10

1. 4/7 - 2/7 =

    (A) 3/7   (B) 6/7   (C) 2   (D) 2/7

2. 1/4 + 1/8 =

    (F) 3/8   (G) 1/6   (H) 2/12   (J) 5/16

3. Diane is having a party. For a bowl of mixed nuts, she already used a 1/2 pound of peanuts, 1/2 pound of walnuts, 3/4 pound of raisins, 2/3 pound of pecans. If she wanted to double the recipe, how many more pounds of peanuts would she need to buy?

    (A) 1/2 pound   (B) 1 pound   (C) 1 1/2 pounds   (D) 1/4 pound

4. Bill, the janitor, glued two sheets of plywood together for strength. One sheet was 1/32 of an inch thick, and the other was 13/32 of an inch thick. How thick was the new board?

    (F) 7/32 inch   (G) 7/16 inch   (H) 13/1024 inch   (J) 3/8 inch

5. 3/4 - 1/2 =

    (A) 2/2   (B) 4/6   (C) 1/4   (D) 3/8

6. 1/3 + 2/9 =

    (F) 1/8   (G) 1/9   (H) 2/3   (J) 5/9

7. 33/12 - 3/4 =

    (A) 30/12   (B) 30/8   (C) 1 9/12   (D) 2

8. Maggie is getting ready for the one-mile race in June. The first day of practice she ran 1/3 of a mile; the second day she ran 1/2 mile; the third day she ran 5/8 of a mile. Which is closest to her total mileage for the three days?

    (F) 1 1/4 miles   (G) 1 1/2 miles   (H) 1 1/8 miles   (J) 1 3/4 miles

 STOP

Mathematics: Geometry

Directions: Read each question, and find the correct answer. Fill in the answer circle for your choice.

Sample

A. Which pair of lines is parallel?

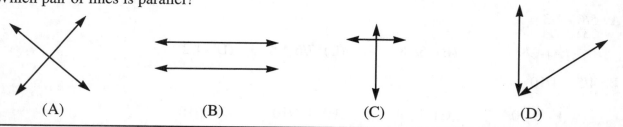

(A)   (B)   (C)   (D)

1. Identify the polygon.

   (A) pentagon   (C) quadrilateral

   (B) hexagon   (D) octagon

2. What is the perimeter of this polygon if all sides are equal?

   (F) 36 feet   (H) 32 feet

   (G) 24 feet   (J) 16 feet

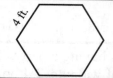

3. What is the diameter of the circle?

   (A) 36 in.   (C) 18.35 in.

   (B) 12 in.   (D) 24 in.

4. How can the triangle be classified?

   (F) obtuse isosceles

   (G) obtuse scalene

   (H) right isosceles

   (J) right scalene

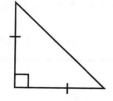

5. Classify triangle EFG.

   (A) isosceles

   (B) scalene

   (C) equilateral

   (D) none of these

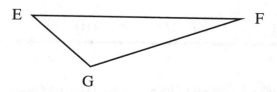

6. Classify the angle below as acute, obtuse, or right.

   (F) acute

   (G) not enough information

   (H) obtuse

   (J) right

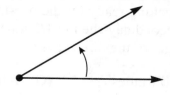

GO →

7. Use the figure. What is the location of point A?

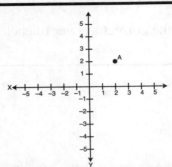

(A) (1,2)

(B) (1,1)

(C) (2,2)

(D) (2,1)

8. Which of these is a right angle?

  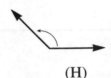 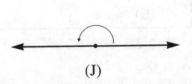

(F) (G) (H) (J)

9. Which of these is a cone?

   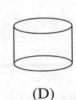

(A) (B) (C) (D)

10. To what number is the arrow pointing?

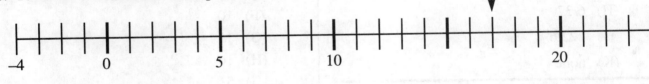

(F) 12   (G) -26   (H) 17   (J) 13

11. Describe how $\overleftrightarrow{UV}$ and $\overleftrightarrow{WX}$ are related.

(A) They are intersecting lines.

(B) They are perpendicular lines.

(C) They are supplementary lines.

(D) They are parallel lines.

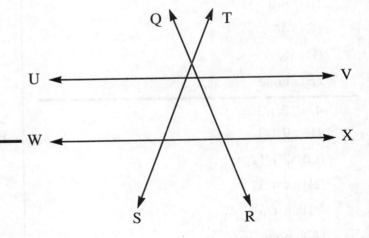

12. Describe how $\overleftrightarrow{QR}$ and $\overleftrightarrow{ST}$ are related.

(F) They are complementary lines.

(G) They are perpendicular lines.

(H) They are intersecting lines.

(J) They are parallel.

➤ STOP ◄

Mathematics: Multiplication—Mixed Numbers

Directions: Fill in the circle for the correct answer to each multiplication problem. Choose "none" if the right answer is not given.

Samples

A. 2 2/7 x 3 1/5 =

  (A) 4

  (B) 2 2/3

  (C) 4/5

  (D) 7 11/35

  (E) none

B. 4 4/5 x 5 3/4 =

  (F) 20 3/5

  (G) 27 3/5

  (H) 28 4/5

  (J) 26 2/5

  (K) none

1. 2 2/5 x 1 1/2 =

  (A) 2 2/5

  (B) 3 1/5

  (C) 2 3/5

  (D) 3 3/5

  (E) none

2. 6 x 1/37 =

  (F) 1/222

  (G) 6/222

  (H) 6/37

  (J) 222/6

  (K) none

3. 8/27 x 3 =

  (A) 8/27

  (B) 9/8

  (C) 4/9

  (D) 8/9

  (E) none

4. 4 x 2 1/3 =

  (F) 9 1/2

  (G) 2 1/12

  (H) 4 4/3

  (J) 8 1/3

  (K) none

5. 2 2/3 x 1/4 =

  (A) 2/3

  (B) 3/4

  (C) 1/4

  (D) 2

  (E) none

6. There are 20 people on your baseball team. One-fourth of the team was chosen to play on an all-star team at the end of the season. How many were chosen?

  (F) 10

  (G) 15

  (H) 16

  (J) 5

  (K) none

7. 2 1/5 x 2/3 =

  (A) 15/22

  (B) 22/15

  (C) 10

  (D) 3/10

  (E) none

Find the product. Simplify if necessary.

8. 2 4/5 x 3/4 =

  (F) 16/15

  (G) 2 1/10

  (H) 2 15/16

  (J) 5/3

  (K) none

➤ **STOP** ◄

Directions: Read each problem. Look for the best answer. Fill in the answer circle for your choice.

Sample

A. If you spin the spinner, what is the probability of the pointer landing on Y?

    (A) 1   (B) 0   (C) 1/8   (D) 1/2

---

1. If you spin the spinner, what is the probability of the pointer landing on G?

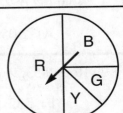

    (A) 1/2   (B) 1/8   (C) 1   (D) 1/4

---

2. If you spin the spinner, what is the probability of the pointer landing on R?

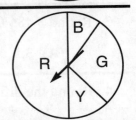

    (F) 1   (G) 1/2   (H) 3/8   (J) 1/4

---

3. Two dice are rolled. Find the probability of rolling a total of 3.

    (A) 1/9   (B) 1/18   (C) 1/36   (D) 1

---

4. A single die is tossed. Find the probability of obtaining a number other than 9.

    (F) 5/6   (G) 1/6   (H) 1   (J) 1/2

---

5. A single die is tossed. Find the probability of obtaining a number greater than 4.

    (A) 5/6   (B) 1/3   (C) 1/6   (D) 1

---

6. The probability of an event happening is 0.75. Which word would you use to describe the probability of the event happening?

    (F) not likely   (G) likely   (H) certain   (J) impossible

---

➤ **STOP** ◄

Directions: Fill in the circle for the correct answer to each rounding problem.

Sample

A. Round 0.557155 to the ten thousandths place.

    (A) 0.55717   (B) 0.55716   (C) 0.5572   (D) 0.5571

---

1. Round 2.0526 to the thousandths place.

    (A) 2.053   (B) 2.05   (C) 2.1   (D) 2.052

---

2. Round 53.26 centimeters to the nearest centimeter.

    (F) 532   (G) 53   (H) 53.3   (J) 54

---

3. Round 3.486 to the ones place.

    (A) 3.5   (B) 3.0   (C) 4.0   (D) 3.4

---

4. Round the difference to the tens place.

$$38.35$$
$$- 12.64$$

    (F) 45   (G) 30   (H) 50   (J) 40

---

5. Round 0.735741 to the hundredths place.

    (A) 0.74   (B) 0.73   (C) 0.737   (D) 0.736

---

6. Round 0.346516 to the tenths place.

    (F) 0.2   (G) 0.3   (H) 0.35   (J) 0.36

---

7. Round the difference to the tens place.

$$60.21$$
$$- 18.71$$

    (A) 55   (B) 50   (C) 30   (D) 40

---

8. Round 2.336 meters to the nearest tenth of a meter.

    (F) 2.4 meters   (G) 2.34 meters (H) 2.3 meters (J) 2.35 meters

---

➤ **STOP** ◄

Mathematics: Operations with Whole Numbers

Directions: Mark the space for the correct answer to each problem. Choose "none of these" if the right answer is not given.

Samples

A.

$$25 \times 4$$

(A) 27
(B) 40
(C) 90
(D) 310
(E) none of these

B.

$$24 \div 8 =$$

(F) 4
(G) 3
(H) 6
(J) 2
(K) none of these

1.

$$417 + 188$$

(A) 605
(B) 591
(C) 606
(D) 695
(E) none of these

5.

$$\begin{array}{r} 4 \\ 12 \\ 59 \\ + 9 \end{array}$$

(A) 72
(B) 82
(C) 71
(D) 62
(E) none of these

2.

$$12 \div 2 =$$

(F) 10
(G) 6
(H) 8
(J) 7
(K) none of these

6.

$$184 + 50 + 16 =$$

(F) 184
(G) 250
(H) 258
(J) 130
(K) none of these

3.

$$\begin{array}{r} 3,418 \\ 502 \\ + 12 \end{array}$$

(A) 3,930
(B) 3,932
(C) 3,922
(D) 39,220
(E) none of these

7.

$$600 \div 2 =$$

(A) 300
(B) 3
(C) 30
(D) 400
(E) none of these

4.
At a football game, 1,364 people sat in the grandstands. Two hundred more stood by the fence and watched. How many saw the game?

(F) 1,564
(G) 1,164
(H) 1,664
(J) 1,500
(K) none of these

8.

What is the average of 8, 12, and 16?

(F) 4
(G) 12
(H) 8
(J) 36
(K) none of these

GO →

Mathematics: Operations with Whole Numbers (cont.)

9.

$2 \times 5 \times 4 =$

(A) 18
(B) 40
(C) 11
(D) 28
(E) none of these

10.

$$\begin{array}{r} 16 \\ \times\ 22 \\ \hline \end{array}$$

(F) 42
(G) 332
(H) 432
(J) 342
(K) none of these

11.

Four girls in two houses are each six years old. How would you show this as a multiplication problem that equals 24 years?

(A) 2×4
(B) $2 \times 4 \times 6$
(C) 4×6
(D) 8×6
(E) none of these

12.

$350 \div 10 =$

(F) 3,500
(G) 35
(H) 35.1
(J) 450
(K) none of these

13.

$137 \times 20 =$

(A) 2,817
(B) 157
(C) 274
(D) 2,740
(E) none of these

14.

$67 \times 5 =$

(F) 72
(G) 335
(H) 62
(J) 330
(K) none of these

15.

There are only 101 chairs set up in the gym for the play. Three times that many are needed for the audience. How many are needed?

(A) 301
(B) 333
(C) 303
(D) 104
(E) none of these

16.

$432 \div 12 =$

(F) 40 r 2
(G) 306
(H) 362
(J) 36
(K) none of these

17.

$$\begin{array}{r} 1{,}137 \\ \times\ 6 \\ \hline \end{array}$$

(A) 1,822
(B) 1,143
(C) 6,822
(D) 6,693
(E) none of these

18.

Average these numbers: 7, 3, 11.

(F) 3
(G) 7
(H) 21
(J) 13
(K) none of these

19.

$90 \div 30 =$

(A) 30
(B) 3
(C) 60
(D) 6
(E) none of these

20.

$$\begin{array}{r} 2{,}334 \\ -\ 135 \\ \hline \end{array}$$

(F) 2,199
(G) 2,101
(H) 2,201
(J) 2,109
(K) none of these

➤ **STOP** ◄

Introduction

Science tries to uncover the physical truth about the way things work—how the seasons change, why animals hibernate, or what kinds of rock are created by volcanoes, for example. To perform your best on questions about science, you must pay attention to important words in each question that might make the answer choices true or untrue.

Here's the Idea

People who work in science try to find out what is true and what is untrue. Questions on science tests often have words in them, such as *not, but, except, always, never,* and *only,* which make answer choices true or untrue. You must watch for these key words in the test questions.

However, before we look at these key words, below are some tips that apply to taking any test, whether it is in language arts, math, science, or social studies. These tips will be repeated because they are important!

Test-Taking Tips

- **Read directions carefully before marking any test questions**, even though you have done that kind of test before. You may think you already know what the directions say, but don't ignore them—read them over. If you don't understand the directions, raise your hand and ask for help. Although your teacher must read the directions exactly as they are written, the teacher can make sure you understand what the directions mean.

- **Follow instructions.** Pay close attention to the sample exercises. They will help you understand what the items on the test will be like and how to mark your answer sheet properly.

- **Read the entire question and all the answer choices.** Do not stop reading when you have found a correct answer. Choices D or E may read "B and D" or "all of the above." On some tests, two answers are both correct. You need to read all the answer choices before marking your answer.

- **For long reading passages, read the questions first so you know what to look for.** If you read the questions first, you'll find information in the passage that answer the questions.

- **Remember that taking a test is not a race!** There are no prizes for finishing first. Use all of the time provided for the test. If you have time left over, check your answers.

Try and Discuss

Let's discuss those key words in many science questions: *not, but, except, always, never,* and *only.*
Words such as *not, but, except, always, never,* and *only* make a big difference, but you must be alert for
these words. Look at these questions.

Which of the following is not part of the circulatory system?

    (A) heart

    (B) bones

    (C) blood vessels

    (D) blood

Fill in the correct circle.

Ⓐ   Ⓑ   Ⓒ   Ⓓ

At first glance, "blood" might seem like the odd one here because it is a liquid; it's not a solid object
like the others. But read the question carefully: "Which of the following is *not* part of the circulatory
system?" It's not asking "Which one does not belong?" The circulatory system does not include bones
so (B) "bones" is the correct answer.

Now look at the following question:

A cabbage has stems and leaves. Which is the only one with scales and bones?

    (A) frog

    (B) cat

    (C) fish

    (D) human

Fill in the correct circle.

Ⓐ   Ⓑ   Ⓒ   Ⓓ

Now, all of these choices have bones, so you may be confused for a moment. But look carefully: the
questions asks, "Which is the *only* one with scales and bones?" Only one choice has both: (C) "fish."

Tips That Help

Remember the following:

- People who work in science try to find out what is true and untrue.

- Pay attention to key words in science questions, such as *not, but, except, always, never,* and *only,*
  that will make answer choices true or untrue.

 Now try the practice tests, listening to your teacher's directions.

Directions: Read each question, and choose the best answer. Fill in the answer for "none of the these" if none of the answers is correct.

> **Sample**
>
> **A.** Where would you find these: bison, coyote, prairie dog?
>   - (A) grassland
>   - (B) desert
>   - (C) tropical forest
>   - (D) deciduous forest
>   - (E) none of these

1. The earth is surrounded by an invisible blanket of air called the
   - (A) stratosphere.
   - (B) ozone layer.
   - (C) atmosphere.
   - (D) subatomic space.
   - (E) none of these.

2. The water droplets in the air are called
   - (F) humidity.
   - (G) gas.
   - (H) temperature.
   - (J) clouds.
   - (K) none of these.

3. Statues, buildings, and people can be harmed by
   - (A) minerals.
   - (B) acid rain.
   - (C) carbon.
   - (D) tar.
   - (E) none of these.

4. A large tropical storm that has very high winds and heavy rainfall is a
   - (F) tornado.
   - (G) hurricane.
   - (H) tidal wave.
   - (J) blizzard.
   - (K) none of these.

5. What is the correct order of the earth's layers, from the surface to the center?
   - (A) core, mantle, crust
   - (B) mantle, core, crust
   - (C) mantle, crust, core
   - (D) crust, mantle, core
   - (E) none of these

6. Which is not caused by the crust of the earth moving?
   - (F) volcanoes
   - (G) earthquakes
   - (H) mountains
   - (J) oceans
   - (K) none of these

GO →

7. Melted material in the earth that cools and hardens is called _____ rock.

   (A) igneous

   (B) metamorphic

   (C) sedimentary

   (D) coal

   (E) none of these

8. Which is not a fossil fuel?

   (F) coal

   (G) oil

   (H) gas

   (J) uranium

   (K) none of these

9. Wind is caused by

   (A) rotation of the sun.

   (B) ocean tides.

   (C) gravity.

   (D) changes in air pressure.

   (E) none of these.

Definitions: Match the column on the left with the choices on the right.

10. erosion	(A) the careful use of natural resources
11. glacier	(B) a reaction in which the nuclei of atoms join together
12. natural resources	(C) a very thin layer of gas high above the earth
13. nuclear fission	(D) a large body of moving ice
14. hydroelectric energy	(F) the trapping and building up of heat in the atmosphere
15. conservation	(G) useful material taken from the environment
16. greenhouse effect	(H) electrical energy produced by moving water
17. ozone layer	(J) the moving away of weathered rock and soil
18. biodegradable substance	(K) a substance that can be broken down by microbes

➤ STOP ◄

Directions: Read the questions, and choose the best answer.

1. The smallest part of an element is
   - (A) an atom.
   - (C) a proton.
   - (B) an electron.
   - (D) a neutron.

2. Which is not a true statement?
   - (F) Objects with opposite charges attract.
   - (G) A magnet is an object that will attract some materials.
   - (H) All atoms attract each other.
   - (J) Objects with the same charge repel, or push away from, each other.

3. When clothes cling together in the dryer or make a crackling sound, this is an example of
   - (A) charging-up.
   - (C) static electricity.
   - (B) proton newness.
   - (D) light being made.

4. Which is an example of a hypothesis?
   - (F) The experiment will take one hour.
   - (G) The experiment will show that plastic is not magnetic.
   - (H) The experiment is about electricity.
   - (J) The experiment needs two partners wearing gloves.

5. For a science fair project, you are going to prove which kind of battery lasts longer—a Glow-on or an Everlight. Which experiment would be the best to prove this?
   - (A) Put the fresh batteries into two different kinds of toys. Turn the toys on. Record which one stops first.
   - (B) Take a Glow-on battery and an Everlight battery from electronic games and test how strong they are.
   - (C) Take two of the same kind of flashlight. Put fresh Glow-on batteries in one and fresh Everlight batteries in the other. Turn both on. Record which one goes out first.
   - (D) Ask people which kind of battery they like and why.

6. Which makes a good insulator?
   - (F) metal wire
   - (G) rubber
   - (H) water
   - (J) glass

7. Magnetic force on Earth is strongest
   - (A) in the oceans.
   - (B) at the North and South Poles.
   - (C) near volcanoes.
   - (D) opposite the moon.

8. The center of an atom is called
   - (F) the proton.
   - (G) the nucleus.
   - (H) the electron.
   - (J) the neutron.

9. The movement of electrons along a path is called
   - (A) a current.
   - (B) a circuit.
   - (C) a field.
   - (D) a site.

10. You can feel the effect of a magnetic field with
    - (F) a compass.
    - (G) a generator.
    - (H) two magnets.
    - (J) a power plant.

➤ **STOP** ◄

Directions: Read the question, and choose the best answer. Fill in the answer for "none of these" if no answer is correct.

Sample

A. The main organ of the nervous system is
(A) the heart.
(B) the brain.
(C) the back bone.
(D) the spinal cord.
(E) none of these.

1. The frame of bones that supports the human body is
(A) the nervous system.
(B) the muscles.
(C) the skeletal system.
(D) the joints.
(E) none of these.

2. Why is marrow important?
(F) It produces new blood cells.
(G) It connects muscles.
(H) It sends signals through the bones.
(J) It rejects poisons.
(K) none of these

3. Where would you not find cartilage?
(A) ears   (D) teeth
(B) nose   (E) none of these
(C) joints

4. Which kind of joint allows you to turn your head from side to side?
(F) sliding
(G) ball-and-socket
(H) hinge
(J) pivot
(K) none of these

5. What stops bones from moving too far apart?
(A) strength   (D) muscles
(B) skin   (E) none of these
(C) other bones

6. An example of an involuntary muscle is
(F) your tongue.
(G) your heart.
(H) your fingers.
(J) your toes.
(K) none of these.

7. A crack or break in a bone is called
(A) a split.
(B) a fragment.
(C) a fracture.
(D) a snap.
(E) none of these.

8. Most of the actions of the body are controlled by
(F) muscles.
(G) the nervous system.
(H) organs.
(J) blood.
(K) none of these.

9. The spinal chord is protected by the
(A) ribs.
(B) backbone.
(C) cerebrum.
(D) organs.
(E) none of these.

10. A quick, automatic reaction is
(F) a nerve.
(G) a muscle twitch.
(H) a reflex.
(J) a thrust.
(K) none of these.

➤ STOP ◄

Directions: Choose the best answer to each question.

Sample

A. Animals without backbones are called
- (A) vertebrates.
- (B) invertebrates.
- (C) environments.
- (D) monerans.

---

1. The arm-like parts of jellyfish and squids are known as
- (A) tentacles.
- (B) antennae.
- (C) stinging cells.
- (D) threads.

2. A living thing that lives on or in another living thing is a
- (F) roundworm.
- (G) planarian.
- (H) parasite.
- (J) snail.

3. Which does not belong?
- (A) earthworm
- (B) leech
- (C) tapeworm
- (D) snake

4. Clams and snails are examples of
- (F) mollusks.
- (G) shrimp.
- (H) fish.
- (J) arachnids.

5. Which doesn't belong?
- (A) bees
- (B) shrimp
- (C) spiders
- (D) starfish

6. To *molt* means
- (F) to hibernate.
- (G) to fly.
- (H) to shed the outer body covering.
- (J) to grow rapidly.

7. Which is not an example of a crustacean?
- (A) lobsters
- (B) earthworm
- (C) crabs
- (D) shrimp

8. Which is not always part of an insect?
- (F) wings
- (G) head
- (H) thorax
- (J) abdomen

9. Spiders and scorpions use _____ to kill insects for food.
- (A) legs
- (B) disease
- (C) poison
- (D) exoskeleton

10. The opening through which water enters a living sponge is a
- (F) ventricle.
- (G) pore.
- (H) mouth.
- (J) tube foot.

➤ **STOP** ◄

Directions: Read the question, and choose the best answer.

Sample

A. Which does not belong?

(A) metals

(B) nonmetals

(C) semimetals

(D) noble gases

---

1. Which does not belong? The common states of matter are

(A) solid.

(B) liquid.

(C) gas.

(D) frozen.

2. When two or more elements combine to form a new substance, it is called a

(F) compound.

(G) metal.

(H) carbon.

(J) gas.

3. A physical property of iron is that it is

(A) not used in computers.

(B) solid.

(C) cheap.

(D) likely to last a long time.

4. Which has the most density?

(F) air

(G) steam

(H) copper

(J) water

5. Which is the best conductor of electricity?

(A) plastic

(B) metal

(C) neon

(D) stone

6. The smallest part of an element is

(F) a model.

(G) an atom.

(H) a particle.

(J) an atomic number.

7. Which does not belong?

(A) molecule

(B) conductivity

(C) chemical bond

(D) atoms joined together

8. What is the chemical symbol for water?

(F) CO_2

(G) H_2O

(H) Wtr

(J) d

9. When liquid gains enough heat, it

(A) melts.

(B) changes to a gas.

(C) freezes.

(D) becomes an element.

10. Materials _____ when cooled.

(F) expand

(G) break

(H) freeze

(J) contract

GO →

---

11. Which property do sugar and salt not have in common?

    (A) crystal

    (B) solid

    (C) electric

    (D) dissolve

12. Iron can be separated from another substance with

    (F) water.

    (G) hydrogen.

    (H) a magnet.

    (J) a high-speed drill.

13. A puddle of water in the sun will

    (A) dissolve.

    (B) change to a solution.

    (C) evaporate.

    (D) spread.

14. The distance an object goes in a certain period of time is its

    (F) motion.

    (G) mass.

    (H) gravity.

    (J) speed.

15. Bicycle brake pads rubbing against a bike tire by squeezing it is an example of

    (A) inertia.

    (B) friction.

    (C) mass.

    (D) force.

16. The force that causes objects to fall and makes the ocean tides is

    (F) the sun.

    (G) power.

    (H) gravity.

    (J) motion.

17. A wooden ball will float when a steel ball of the same size will not. Why?

    (A) The steel will rust.

    (B) Steel goes through water.

    (C) The wooden ball is less dense.

    (D) Gravity makes the difference.

18. _____ acts only on certain materials such as iron, steel, and nickel.

    (F) Friction

    (G) Magnetic force

    (H) Poles

    (J) Buoyant force

➤ STOP ◄

Directions: Read the passage, and choose the best answer for each question.

Scientists study the fossils in rocks to find out how old the rocks are. Fossils give clues about what happened in Earth's history. Fossils are mainly found in rock that used to be mud millions of years ago. Most fossils are of animals with shells and tiny parts of plants and animals. Some fossils are so small they must be studied under a microscope. These are the kind scientists study the most.

The word *fossil* makes many people think of dinosaurs. Dinosaurs appear in books, movies, and television programs. The bones and large fossils of some dinosaurs are in many museums. These reptiles lived on Earth for well over 100 million years. Many dinosaurs were quite small, but some weighed as much as 80 tons! By around 65 million years ago, all dinosaurs were extinct. Why they disappeared and what made them disappear so quickly are unanswered questions.

At one time, scientists did not know which fossils came first. They did not know which animals shown in fossils were older than others. Someone who helped make this clear was William Smith, an English engineer. Smith was in charge of building waterways in England about 100 years ago. He needed to know what kinds of rocks he would have to cut through in hills. Often, he could tell if the rock under the ground was hard or soft by studying fossils lying nearby. Smith knew it was useful to tell how and when rocks were formed. But it was only much later that scientists could explain what fossils could tell us about Earth's history. They continue to do this by putting fossils in order, from the oldest ones to most recent.

1. The correct order of events in this passage is

   1—William Smith made a careful study of fossils.

   2—Scientists continue to put fossils in order.

   3—By 65 million years ago, all dinosaurs were extinct.

   4—Dinosaurs lived on Earth for over 100 million years.

   (A) 4-3-1-2   (C) 2-4-3-1
   (B) 1-2-4-3   (D) 4-3-2-1

2. It is probably true that before William Smith began studying fossils,

   (F) there were no fossils.

   (G) few people understood the meaning of fossils.

   (H) fossils were not put in order.

   (J) G and H

3. Someday, it will be true that

   (A) there will be fossils from our time.

   (B) all fossils will be destroyed.

   (C) William Smith will discover new fossils.

   (D) fossils will not mean anything.

4. There are many fossils of tiny animals because

   (F) there were only tiny animals millions of years ago.

   (G) their bodies became trapped in mud.

   (H) fossils of tiny animals are the only kind of fossils.

   (J) no one is interested in large fossils.

5. Which details best support the idea that tiny fossils are of creatures who have lived in water?

   (A) Fossils are found in rock that used to be mud.

   (B) Some fossils are so small they must be studied under a microscope.

   (C) Most fossils are of animals with shells.

   (D) Smith was in charge of building waterways.

6. The best title for this passage would be

   (F) Fossils and Dinosaurs: What's the Difference?

   (G) How Old Are Rocks?

   (H) Fossils: Clues to Earth's History.

   (J) The Man Who Discovered Fossils.

➤ **STOP** ◄

Directions: Read the passage, and answer the questions. If none of the answers are correct, fill in the letter for "none of these."

The ground shakes when the crust of the earth moves. This is called an earthquake. It can be caused by the crust sliding, volcanic bursts, or manmade explosions. Earthquakes that cause the most damage come from the crust sliding.

At first, the crust may only bend because of pushing forces. When the pushing becomes too much, the crust snaps and shifts into a new position. Shifting makes wiggles of energy that go out in all directions, like ripples when a stone is dropped in water. These are called "seismic waves." The waves travel out from the center of the earthquake. Sometimes people can hear these waves. This is because they make the whole planet ring like a bell. It must be awesome to hear this sound!

The crust moving may leave a crack, or fault, in the land. Geologists, scientists who study the earth's surface, say that earthquakes often happen where there are old faults. These are weak places in the crust. Where there are faults, earthquakes may happen again and again.

When earthquakes happen under the ocean floor, they sometimes cause huge sea waves. These waves travel across the ocean as fast as 597 miles per hour and may be 49 feet high or higher. During the 1964 Alaskan earthquake, giant waves caused most of the damage to the towns of Kodiak, Cordova, and Seward. Some waves raced across the ocean in the other direction to the coasts of Japan.

Although earthquakes are usually frightening, keep in mind that the distance to the center of the earth is 3,960 miles. Most earthquakes begin less than 150 miles below the surface. Earthquakes are not a sign that the planet is unsteady.

1. According to the passage, earthquakes can be caused by
   (A) a giant sound under the ground.
   (B) explosions and the crust sliding.
   (C) volcanoes.
   (D) B and C.
   (E) none of these.

2. Huge waves that race across the ocean can be caused by
   (F) storms.
   (G) damage.
   (H) earthquakes under the ocean.
   (J) waves as high as 49 feet.
   (K) none of these.

3. Seismic waves are compared to
   (A) ripples in water.
   (B) sounds.
   (C) a bell ringing.
   (D) faults in the ground.
   (E) none of these.

4. Which of these is an opinion?
   (F) The ground shakes when the crust of the earth moves.
   (G) It must be awesome to hear this sound!
   (H) Where there are faults, earthquakes may happen again and again.
   (J) Most earthquakes begin less than 150 miles below the surface.
   (K) none of these

GO →

5. According to the passage, a possible effect of earthquakes is that they can create
   (A) faults, or cracks, in the ground.
   (B) volcanic bursts.
   (C) a crack that is 3,960 miles long and goes to the center of the earth.
   (D) a stone dropped in water.
   (E) none of these.

6. The author's purpose in this passage is
   (F) to entertain.
   (G) to persuade.
   (H) to inform.
   (J) to excuse.
   (K) none of these.

7. When earthquakes happen under the ocean floor, they sometimes cause huge sea waves. This is probably caused by
   (A) cracks in the ocean floor.
   (B) wiggles of energy.
   (C) loud noises.
   (D) weak places in the crust.
   (E) none of these.

8. Which is the correct order of events in an earthquake?
   1—The planet rings like a bell.
   2—The crust bends and snaps.
   3—Pushing forces build up under the crust.
   4—Energy is released as seismic waves.
   (F) 4-3-2-1
   (G) 1-3-2-4
   (H) 3-2-4-1
   (J) 3-4-2-1
   (K) 2-1-3-4

9. You read in the newspaper that an old fault has been discovered nearby. What may happen?
   (A) It will close up someday.
   (B) An earthquake may happen there.
   (C) People will hear seismic waves coming from it.
   (D) Earthquakes will come from much deeper there.
   (E) none of these

10. A good title for this passage would be
    (F) Giant Waves from Nowhere.
    (G) How Earthquakes Happen.
    (H) The Mysteries of Our Earth.
    (J) Stay Put When Earthquakes Happen!
    (K) Earthquakes in Japan.

➤ STOP ≺

Directions: Choose the best answer for each question.

Sample

A. What type of organism causes bread to rise?

    (A) fungi   (B) monerans   (C) viruses   (D) nucleus   (E) none of these

---

Match the items on the left with the definitions on the right.

    1. another name for monerans   (A) virus

    2. the basic part of all living things   (B) fungi

    3. a plant-like living thing that does not contain chlorophyll   (C) organism

    4. any single living thing   (D) bacteria

    5. a thing that seems to be alive but is not made of cells   (E) cell

---

Use the terms below to complete the paragraph.

       (F) cell wall   (G) cytoplasm   (H) kingdoms   (J) protists   (K) nucleus

Scientists classify all organisms into five _____ 6 _____. The one-celled

organisms make up the kingdom of _____ 7 _____. Like all cells, these

have a _____ 8 _____ or control center. The _____ 9 _____

goes around the edge of the cell. Inside is the _____ 10 _____, a jelly-like

material surrounding the nucleus.

---

11. A green substance found in plants which is needed for making food is

    (A) fungi.   (B) leaves.   (C) cells.   (D) chlorophyll.   (E) amebas.

---

12. AIDS is an example of a

    (F) bacteria.   (G) virus.   (H) fungi.   (J) spore.   (K) organism.

➤ **STOP** ◄

Science: The Solar System

Directions: Read the questions, and choose the best answer.

1. Which words belong together?
   - (A) star, sun, crater, water
   - (B) comet, tail, ice, light
   - (C) star, comet, blast, rings
   - (D) Mars, sunspots, rocket, ice

2. Sun is to star as Earth is to
   - (F) moon.
   - (G) orbit.
   - (H) planet.
   - (J) bright.

3. Which picture shows the correct position of Earth, the sun, and the moon during a solar eclipse?

Key
Earth (O)
sun (O)
moon (o)

   - (A) O O o
   - (B) O O o
   - (C) o O O
   - (D) O o O

4. The center of the solar system is
   - (F) Earth.
   - (G) the sun.
   - (H) the Milky Way.
   - (J) the universe.

5. How long is a day on Earth?
   - (A) 12 hours
   - (B) 24 hours
   - (C) 10 hours
   - (D) 8 hours

6. When Earth receives the most direct sunlight, it is
   - (F) winter.
   - (G) spring.
   - (H) summer.
   - (J) fall.

7. The planet with rings in our solar system is
   - (A) Pluto
   - (B) Mars.
   - (C) the sun.
   - (D) Saturn.

8. Meteorites striking the surface of the moon cause
   - (F) volcanoes.
   - (G) craters.
   - (H) dust storms.
   - (J) magnetism.

9. The greatest number of sunspots have appeared on the sun in these years:
   1946 1957 1968 1979 1990

   If the pattern continues, predict when the greatest number of sunspots will appear again.
   - (A) 1999
   - (B) 2001
   - (C) 2068
   - (D) 1998

10. The planets stay in orbit because of
    - (F) size.
    - (G) speed.
    - (H) atmosphere.
    - (J) gravity.

➤ STOP ◄

Introduction

Social studies is all about people and places. It can be difficult at times to remember many names and events. But to perform your best on a social studies section, it helps to ask yourself a question about the question!

Here's the Idea

A social studies question may be about a region, a president, or an event. It helps focus your attention on what the question is asking—and it helps you eliminate choices, too—if you ask yourself *who, what, where, when,* or *how.*

However, before we look at these key words, below are some tips that apply to taking any test, whether it is in language arts, math, science, or social studies. These tips are repeated because they are important!

Test-Taking Tips

- **Read directions carefully before marking any test questions**, even though you have done that kind of test before. You may think you already know what the directions say, but don't ignore them—read them over. If you don't understand the directions, raise your hand and ask for help. Although your teacher must read the directions exactly as they are written, the teacher can make sure you understand what the directions mean.

- **Follow instructions.** Pay close attention to the sample exercises. They will help you understand what the items on the test will be like and how to mark your answer sheet properly.

- **Read the entire question and all the answer choices.** Do not stop reading when you have found a correct answer. Choices D or E may read "B and D" or "all of the above." On some tests, two answers are both correct. You need to read all the answer choices before marking your answer.

- **For long reading passages, read the questions first so you know what to look for.** If you read the questions first, you'll find information in the passage that answer the questions.

- **Remember that taking a test is not a race!** There are no prizes for finishing first. Use all of the time provided for the test. If you have time left over, check your answers.

Try and Discuss

Let's discuss asking the questions *who, what, where, when,* or *how.* Social studies questions are about persons, places, or events and when or how they happened.

For example, here's a social studies test question:

A major industry of the Midwest region is

Fill in the correct circle.

(A) agriculture.
(B) Illinois, Ohio, Wisconsin, Iowa, and Michigan.
(C) fishing.
(D) the Civil War.

Ask yourself, "Is this a question about *who, what, where, when,* or *how?*" It asks about "a major industry." It is asking *what,* <u>not</u> *where,* which eliminates choice (B) right away. The correct answer is (A) "agriculture."

Look at the list of topics below. Would they probably be asking *who, what, where, when,* or *how?* (You may be right sometimes if you suggest more than one.)

- maps

- climate

- resources

- people

- history

Tips That Help

Social studies is all about people and places. It can be difficult at times to remember lots of names and events. But to perform your best on a social studies section, it helps to ask yourself a question about the question: *who, what, where, when,* or *how.*

Now try the practice tests, listening to your teacher's directions.

Directions: Match the terms on the left with their definitions on the right.

Terms	Definitions
1. veto	(A) a statement added to change the Constitution
2. civil rights	(B) the rejection of a law passed by a lawmaking body
3. amendment	(C) the eleven states that seceded from the United States
4. Confederacy	(D) the individual freedoms of each citizen

Terms	Definitions
5. emancipation	(F) a group of people who move as the seasons change
6. immigrant	(G) a product sold by one country to another
7. nomads	(H) the act of freeing people from unjust control
8. export	(J) a person who leaves his or her country to live in another

Terms	Definitions
9. patriotism	(A) information about events recorded when the events occurred
10. primary source	(B) a large farm with workers where one crop is grown
11. reform	(C) a change for the better
12. plantation	(D) the love and loyal support for one's country

Terms	Definitions
13. segregation	(F) the right to vote
14. treaty	(G) a written or spoken agreement, especially between nations
15. colony	(H) a territory under the rule of another country
16. suffrage	(J) the policy of keeping people of different races apart

> STOP <

Directions: Read the questions below. Each will ask you to put people or events in the correct order. Choose the best answer.

Sample

A. 1-John F. Kennedy
2-Abraham Lincoln
3-Thomas Jefferson
4-Jimmy Carter

Put the presidents in order from 1801–1977.

(A) 1-2-4-3

(B) 2-1-3-4

(C) 4-3-2-1

(D) 3-2-1-4

1. 1-The North and South fight each other in the Civil War.
2-British troops kill American civilians in the Boston Massacre.
3-Christopher Columbus sails from Spain to the Western Hemisphere.
4-The Pilgrims found Plymouth Colony.

Which is the correct order of events?

(A) 2-3-1-4

(B) 3-4-2-1

(C) 1-3-2-1

(D) 3-2-1-4

2. 1-The U.S. spacecraft *Challenger* explodes, killing all seven crew members.
2-Gold discovered in California triggers the Gold Rush.
3-World War I is started by the assassination of Archduke Ferdinand.
4-The Founding Fathers write the Constitution.

Which is the correct order of events?

(F) 4-3-2-1

(G) 3-2-1-4

(H) 2-3-4-1

(J) 4-2-3-1

3. 1-Lewis & Clark
2-Samuel de Champlain
3-Ferdinand Magellan
4-Neil Armstrong

Which is the correct order of explorers?

(A) 2-3-1-4   (C) 3-2-1-4

(B) 1-2-3-4   (D) 3-1-2-4

4. 1-Richard M. Nixon
2-Andrew Jackson
3-Ronald W. Reagan
4-Ulysses S. Grant

Put the presidents in order from 1829–1981.

(F) 2-1-3-4   (H) 1-3-2-4

(G) 2-4-1-3   (J) 3-4-1-2

5. 1-Pony Express riders begin carrying mail to the Far West.
2-World War II begins with Hitler's invasion of Poland.
3-The Revolutionary War between the colonists and the British begins with the Declaration of Independence.
4-Martin Luther King, Jr. organizes marches against discrimination.

Which is the correct order of events?

(A) 4-2-3-1

(B) 1-3-2-4

(C) 3-2-1-4

(D) 3-1-2-4

6. 1-The Twenty-Sixth Amendment to the Bill of Rights
2-The Declaration of Independence
3-The Emancipation Proclamation
4-The Constitution of the United States

(F) 4-3-2-1

(G) 2-4-3-1

(H) 4-2-1-3

(J) 2-1-3-4

> **STOP** <

Social Studies: Famous Persons

Directions: Read the name of the person, and choose the correct identification.

Sample

A. Abraham Lincoln
- (A) president during the Civil War
- (B) signer of the Declaration of Independence
- (C) first president of the United States
- (D) Union general

1. Robert E. Lee
   - (A) president of the Confederacy
   - (B) American portrait painter
   - (C) 22nd president of the United States
   - (D) American Confederate general

2. Patrick Henry
   - (F) Spanish explorer
   - (G) famous speechmaker during the American Revolution
   - (H) inventor of the steamboat
   - (J) King of England, 1603–1625

3. Crispus Attucks
   - (A) American frontiersman
   - (B) former slave killed in the Boston Massacre
   - (C) African-American scientist
   - (D) American Northwest explorer

4. Sacajawea
   - (F) American abolitionist
   - (G) American slave who sued for her freedom
   - (H) Indian chief and friend of the Pilgrims
   - (J) Shoshone Indian guide who aided Lewis and Clark

5. Nat Turner
   - (A) American leader of a slave revolt
   - (B) American frontiersman
   - (C) African-American scientist
   - (D) Mormon religious leader

6. Elizabeth Cady Stanton
   - (F) American Civil War heroine
   - (G) American abolitionist and social reformer
   - (H) Queen of England, 1533–1603
   - (J) American first lady, wife of James Madison

7. Benjamin Franklin
   - (A) Union general
   - (B) English explorer
   - (C) 16th U.S. president
   - (D) American statesman, scientist, and journalist

8. Montezuma
   - (F) Spanish explorer
   - (G) last Aztec emperor in Mexico
   - (H) Nez Perce leader
   - (J) Portuguese explorer

9. Dred Scott
   - (A) American slave who sued for his freedom
   - (B) author of *Uncle Tom's Cabin*
   - (C) author of the first American dictionary
   - (D) American inventor of the cotton gin

10. Harriet Beecher Stowe
    - (F) author of *Uncle Tom's Cabin*
    - (G) American feminist
    - (H) American Indian princess
    - (J) American revolutionary heroine

➤ **STOP** ◄

Directions: Read the name of the location, and choose the correct identification.

Sample

A. Cape Cod

  (A) tip of South America

  (B) site of space shuttle launchings

  (C) landing place of Pilgrims on the *Mayflower*

  (D) waterway connecting Arctic Ocean and Bering Sea

---

1. Fort Sumter

  (A) site of General Robert E. Lee's surrender

  (B) site of first Civil War battle

  (C) capital of Massachusetts

  (D) fort in Kentucky founded by Daniel Boone

2. Erie Canal

  (F) pass through the Appalachian Mountains into Tennessee

  (G) named for explorer Henry Hudson

  (H) artificial waterway in New York, 525 miles long

  (J) one of the five Great Lakes

3. District of Columbia

  (A) site of U.S. capital

  (B) capital of Ohio

  (C) group of islands in the Atlantic Ocean

  (D) same as the Northwest Territory

4. Jamestown

  (F) largest city in the state of New York

  (G) site of the first Civil War battle

  (H) capital of Rhode Island

  (J) first permanent English settlement in America

5. Lexington

  (A) capital of Massachusetts

  (B) site of first battle between colonists and British troops

  (C) port city in South Carolina on Atlantic Ocean

  (D) fort that later became Chicago, Illinois

6. Louisiana Territory

  (F) also known as Oregon Territory

  (G) city at the mouth of the Mississippi

  (H) deep canyon in Arizona

  (J) western half of Mississippi River basin purchased from France

7. Valley Forge

  (A) George Washington's winter camp in 1777

  (B) longest mountain range in the United States

  (C) large, flat, dry area in the western United States

  (D) site of the first United States capital

8. New Amsterdam

  (F) largest city in Louisiana

  (G) founded by the Dutch; now New York City

  (H) part of the Appalachian Mountains in New York

  (J) fishing area off Newfoundland

9. Philadelphia

  (A) capital of Virginia

  (B) location of the Constitutional Convention

  (C) capital of England

  (D) capital of Georgia

10. Plymouth

  (F) capital of California

  (G) George Washington's winter camp in 1777

  (H) largest city in Michigan

  (J) site of the first Pilgrim settlement

➤ **STOP** ◄

Social Studies: Maps and Globes

Directions: Read the questions, and choose the best answer.

Samples

A. Which is not a Southwestern state?
- (A) Texas
- (B) Oregon
- (C) Arizona
- (D) New Mexico

B. Which is the smallest continent?
- (F) North America
- (G) Australia
- (H) Africa
- (J) Asia

1. How would you best describe a continent?
   - (A) mountains, valleys, and streams
   - (B) a globe
   - (C) a large land mass
   - (D) a point on a map

2. Which pair does not belong?
   - (F) latitude, longitude
   - (G) high, low
   - (H) degrees, minutes
   - (J) Eastern Hemisphere, Western Hemisphere

3. Which of the following is not a continent?
   - (A) Canada
   - (B) South America
   - (C) Australia
   - (D) Antarctica

4. The Northern and the Southern Hemispheres are divided by
   - (F) the prime meridian.
   - (G) water.
   - (H) longitude.
   - (J) the equator.

5. The United States is located _____ of Central America.
   - (A) south
   - (B) north
   - (C) west
   - (D) east

6. The United States is bounded by these bodies of water except
   - (F) the Pacific Ocean.
   - (G) the Atlantic Ocean.
   - (H) the Gulf of Mexico.
   - (J) the Indian Ocean.

7. The Great Lakes are on the border of
   - (A) the state of Alaska and Canada.
   - (B) Mexico and the United States.
   - (C) Canada and the United States.
   - (D) the United States and the Arctic.

8. Which of the following is a true statement?
   - (F) A region is an area that shares a mountain range.
   - (G) Each state in the United States is a region.
   - (H) A region is an area of land that has one or more characteristics in common.
   - (J) The Mississippi River divides the United States into two regions, East and West.

9. On a climate map you would expect to see
   - (A) natural resources.
   - (B) temperature.
   - (C) favorite vacation spots.
   - (D) average depth of bodies of water.

10. Which is not a natural boundary?
    - (F) a mountain range
    - (G) a highway
    - (H) a coastline
    - (J) a river

11. The number of people in a region is its
    - (A) population.
    - (B) census.
    - (C) democracy.
    - (D) mass.

12. The United States shares its longest border with
    - (F) New England.
    - (G) Canada.
    - (H) Mexico.
    - (J) Central America.

➤ **STOP** ◄

Social Studies: United States History

Directions: Read the questions, and choose the best answer. Fill in "none of these" if none of the answers is correct.

1. Why did the first groups of English settlers come to the New World?
   - (A) to look for gold
   - (B) to spread their religion around the world
   - (C) to find a new route to the East Indies
   - (D) to practice their religion openly
   - (E) none of these

2. The original thirteen states had been _____ of Great Britain.
   - (F) territories
   - (G) regions
   - (H) kingdoms
   - (J) colonies
   - (K) none of these

3. The most important cause of the American Revolution was
   - (A) the price of goods in Boston was too high.
   - (B) England was too far away to communicate with.
   - (C) whaling was too difficult at which to make a living.
   - (D) Americans were not represented in England's government.
   - (E) none of these.

4. Where was the Declaration of Independence signed?
   - (F) New York City
   - (G) Washington, D.C.
   - (H) Boston, Massachusetts
   - (J) Philadelphia, Pennsylvania
   - (K) none of these

5. The purpose of building canals was to
   - (A) move people faster than the railroad could.
   - (B) speed the movement of people and products.
   - (C) irrigate farmlands.
   - (D) spread fishing throughout the states.
   - (E) none of these.

6. Which of the following is an example of an import?
   - (F) a car made in Germany and shipped to New York
   - (G) corn sent from Illinois to Russia
   - (H) glass sent from Pittsburgh to Detroit
   - (J) computers made in California and sold in stores
   - (K) none of these

GO →

7. Why is Washington, D.C., in the District of Columbia?

   (A) The district is land not part of any state.

   (B) The district is in the middle of the nation.

   (C) The district is near the Atlantic Ocean for travel.

   (D) The district is just the right size for the national capital.

   (E) none of these

8. Which event led to the start of the Civil War?

   (F) Escaped slaves revolted in the South.

   (G) Abraham Lincoln was elected president.

   (H) The Southern states formed a Confederacy.

   (J) Southern troops fired on Fort Sumter.

   (K) none of these

9. Why did New Orleans become a major center of trade?

   (A) It is located near major water routes.

   (B) It is located in the Deep South.

   (C) It was not involved in the Civil War.

   (D) It was once part of the French empire.

   (E) none of these

10. What was a major reason people came to California in the mid-1800s?

    (F) freedom

    (G) the discovery of gold

    (H) the discovery of oil

    (J) whaling

    (K) none of these

11. What means of transportation made travel to the West much faster after the Civil War?

    (A) steamships

    (B) railroads

    (C) airplanes

    (D) sailing ships

    (E) none of these

12. Native Americans, surrounded by settlers coming West, were moved by the United States government to

    (F) plantations.

    (G) national parks.

    (H) canyons.

    (J) reservations.

    (K) none of these.

➤ STOP ◄

Directions: Read the passage, and choose the best answer to each question.

Gold!

The story of United States gold is nearly as old as the United States itself. Gold was produced in the southern Appalachian Mountains as early as 1792. It may have been mined as early as 1775 in what is now southern California, too. But the big boom in gold mining came shortly before the Civil War. The discovery of gold at Sutter's Mill in California sparked the Gold Rush of 1849–50. Hundreds of mining camps sprang to life as new deposits were discovered. But how did ordinary people get into the business of finding gold in those years? Was gold just lying around on the ground?

Gold resists weathering very well. It doesn't rust or dissolve easily. When freed from rocks, gold is carried downstream as particles of "dust," flakes, grains, or nuggets. Fine gold particles collect in dips or in pockets in sand and gravel where the stream current slows down. Concentrations of gold in gravel are called "pay streaks." In gold-bearing country, prospectors look for gold where coarse sands and gravel are thick on the bottom of the stream bed.

During the Gold Rush, the equipment used by many prospectors was simple: just a wide, flat pan. Prospectors would scoop up small amounts of water and sand or gravel in the pan, swish it around, and look for bits of gold. It was a slow process, but stories of prospectors finding thousands of dollars of gold in a single week were common. Unfortunately, as you might expect, there were also fights, robberies, and even murders connected with prospecting.

Gold production increased rapidly as settlers moved West. Huge deposits in California and Nevada were discovered during the 1860s. The Cripple Creek deposits in Colorado began to produce gold in 1892. By 1905, the Tonopah and Goldfield deposits in Nevada and the Alaskan placer deposits had been discovered. The largest gold mine in the United States is the Homestake mine at Lead, South Dakota. This mine, which is 8,000 feet deep, has accounted for almost 10 percent of total United States gold production since it opened in 1876. It's estimated that the mine holds about 40 million ounces of gold. The total output from gold deposits in the United States since 1792 has reached more than 400 million ounces. That may not sound like a lot, but it's enough gold to fill a school gymnasium!

Governments of the world still use gold as a kind of international money because it is valuable everywhere. A large part of the gold stocks of the United States is stored in the vault of the Fort Knox Bullion Depository. The depository is located about 30 miles southwest of Louisville, Kentucky. Inside the vaults of Fort Knox, gold is stacked unwrapped in bars that look like shining bricks. Each one weighs about 27.5 pounds, or about 400 ounces. Figuring that gold is worth approximately $300 an ounce, a single bar has a value of $120,000—probably more than any pay streak ever discovered by a patient prospector panning a stream 150 years ago.

GO →

1. What is the topic sentence of the first paragraph?

   (A) The story of United States gold is nearly as old as the United States itself.

   (B) But the big boom in gold mining came shortly before the Civil War.

   (C) The discovery of gold at Sutter's Mill in California sparked the Gold Rush of 1849–50.

   (D) But how did ordinary people get into the business of finding gold in those years?

2. The main idea of the whole passage is that

   (F) machines succeeded where prospectors failed.

   (G) the United States is the richest country in the world.

   (H) gold mining has become an important part of the United States' economy.

   (J) practically everyone would like to find gold!

3. Which happened first?

   (A) Prospectors report finding thousands of dollars of gold in a single week.

   (B) Gold is produced in the Appalachian Mountains.

   (C) Gold is found at Sutter's Mill.

   (D) Gold mines begin producing gold in great quantities.

4. Which is probably true based on information in the passage?

   (F) Someday gold won't be valuable.

   (G) There is more gold underground than on the surface.

   (H) The gold at Fort Knox is there because it's part of history.

   (J) Gold is popular for jewelry.

5. Which of the following statements is an opinion?

   (A) A single bar has a value of $120,000—probably more than any pay streak ever discovered by a patient prospector panning a stream 150 years ago.

   (B) Gold production increased rapidly as settlers moved West.

   (C) During the Gold Rush, the equipment used by many prospectors was simple: just a wide, flat pan.

   (D) Was gold just lying around on the ground?

6. The author's purpose in this passage is to

   (F) entertain readers with a story about the Old West.

   (G) persuade readers that gold is worth having.

   (H) inform readers about the history of gold production in the United States.

   (J) give his or her opinion about how interesting gold is.

➤ **STOP** ◄

Directions: Choose which concept from the list belongs in the blanks in the passage below.

An American Theme: Freedom

The _____1_____ of the British Empire in the 17th century led to the founding of fishing and

trading villages in North America. Under Britain's control, raw resources from these places were

used to manufacture finished goods and products in the mother country. This practice is called

_____2_____. Another practice that quickly spread to the colonies was _____3_____, which was

supposed to provide cheap labor but which completely denied the rights of the people being

bought and sold. When the colonists revolted against Britain, it was not the rights of the slaves

they were concerned about; it was their own _____4_____. The specific issue that touched off the

Revolutionary War was _____5_____ without representation in Parliament. Colonists had no direct

say in the policies and laws affecting them. The success of the Revolution led slowly to a feeling

of _____6_____ among Americans. They saw themselves as free people who could follow their

own _____7_____. Gradually, Americans moved westward, looking for homes and opportunities

beyond the Appalachian Mountains. But with the issue of slavery still unsettled—a growing

number of people in the North objected to it—every time a state applied for _____8_____ into the

Union, the question of slavery was argued over again. Finally, Southern states left the Union,

arguing that _____9_____ came before federal law. The Civil War was fought over the question of

whether states could leave the Union. During the conflict, slavery was _____10_____ by Congress

and Abraham Lincoln. Still today, individual rights and freedoms are some of the most hotly

debated topics among Americans. They are at the center of the history of the United States.

(A) taxation   (C) slavery   (E) destiny   (G) equality   (J) nationalism

(B) expansion   (D) states' rights   (F) abolished   (H) admission   (K) colonialism

➤ **STOP** ◄

Student Answer Sheets

Language Arts: Synonym Analogies
Test page: 17

Sample

A. Ⓐ Ⓑ Ⓒ Ⓓ

Test

1. Ⓐ Ⓑ Ⓒ Ⓓ
2. Ⓕ Ⓖ Ⓗ Ⓙ
3. Ⓐ Ⓑ Ⓒ Ⓓ
4. Ⓕ Ⓖ Ⓗ Ⓙ
5. Ⓐ Ⓑ Ⓒ Ⓓ
6. Ⓕ Ⓖ Ⓗ Ⓙ
7. Ⓐ Ⓑ Ⓒ Ⓓ
8. Ⓕ Ⓖ Ⓗ Ⓙ

Language Arts: Capitalization
Test page: 18

Samples

A. Ⓐ Ⓑ Ⓒ Ⓓ
B. Ⓕ Ⓖ Ⓗ Ⓙ

Test

1. Ⓐ Ⓑ Ⓒ Ⓓ
2. Ⓕ Ⓖ Ⓗ Ⓙ
3. Ⓐ Ⓑ Ⓒ Ⓓ
4. Ⓕ Ⓖ Ⓗ Ⓙ
5. Ⓐ Ⓑ Ⓒ Ⓓ
6. Ⓕ Ⓖ Ⓗ Ⓙ
7. Ⓐ Ⓑ Ⓒ Ⓓ
8. Ⓕ Ⓖ Ⓗ Ⓙ

Language Arts: Fiction
Test pages: 19–21

Test

1. Ⓐ Ⓑ Ⓒ Ⓓ
2. Ⓕ Ⓖ Ⓗ Ⓙ
3. Ⓐ Ⓑ Ⓒ Ⓓ
4. Ⓕ Ⓖ Ⓗ Ⓙ
5. Ⓐ Ⓑ Ⓒ Ⓓ
6. Ⓕ Ⓖ Ⓗ Ⓙ
7. Ⓐ Ⓑ Ⓒ Ⓓ
8. Ⓕ Ⓖ Ⓗ Ⓙ

Language Arts: Poetry and Verse
Test pages: 22–23

Test

1. Ⓐ Ⓑ Ⓒ Ⓓ
2. Ⓕ Ⓖ Ⓗ Ⓙ
3. Ⓐ Ⓑ Ⓒ Ⓓ
4. Ⓕ Ⓖ Ⓗ Ⓙ
5. Ⓐ Ⓑ Ⓒ Ⓓ
6. Ⓕ Ⓖ Ⓗ Ⓙ
7. _____
8. _____
9. Ⓐ Ⓑ Ⓒ Ⓓ
10. _____

Language Arts: Punctuation
Test page: 24

Sample

A. Ⓐ Ⓑ Ⓒ Ⓓ Ⓔ

Test

1. Ⓐ Ⓑ Ⓒ Ⓓ Ⓔ
2. Ⓕ Ⓖ Ⓗ Ⓙ Ⓚ
3. Ⓐ Ⓑ Ⓒ Ⓓ Ⓔ
4. Ⓕ Ⓖ Ⓗ Ⓙ Ⓚ
5. Ⓐ Ⓑ Ⓒ Ⓓ Ⓔ
6. Ⓕ Ⓖ Ⓗ Ⓙ Ⓚ

Language Arts: Research
Test pages: 25–26

Test

1. Ⓐ Ⓑ Ⓒ Ⓓ
2. Ⓕ Ⓖ Ⓗ Ⓙ
3. Ⓐ Ⓑ Ⓒ Ⓓ
4. Ⓕ Ⓖ Ⓗ Ⓙ
5. Ⓐ Ⓑ Ⓒ Ⓓ
6. Ⓕ Ⓖ Ⓗ Ⓙ
7. Ⓐ Ⓑ Ⓒ Ⓓ
8. Ⓐ Ⓑ
9. Ⓐ Ⓑ
10. Ⓐ Ⓑ
11. Ⓐ Ⓑ
12. Ⓐ Ⓑ
13. Ⓐ Ⓑ Ⓒ Ⓓ
14. Ⓕ Ⓖ Ⓗ Ⓙ
15. Ⓐ Ⓑ Ⓒ Ⓓ
16. Ⓕ Ⓖ Ⓗ Ⓙ

Language Arts: Sentences
Test page: 27

Sample

A. Ⓐ Ⓑ Ⓒ Ⓓ

Test

1. Ⓐ Ⓑ Ⓒ Ⓓ
2. Ⓕ Ⓖ Ⓗ Ⓙ
3. Ⓐ Ⓑ Ⓒ Ⓓ
4. Ⓕ Ⓖ Ⓗ Ⓙ

Language Arts: Spelling
Test page: 28

Samples

A. Ⓐ Ⓑ Ⓒ Ⓓ
B. Ⓕ Ⓖ Ⓗ Ⓙ

Test

1. Ⓐ Ⓑ Ⓒ Ⓓ
2. Ⓕ Ⓖ Ⓗ Ⓙ
3. Ⓐ Ⓑ Ⓒ Ⓓ
4. Ⓕ Ⓖ Ⓗ Ⓙ
5. Ⓐ Ⓑ Ⓒ Ⓓ
6. Ⓕ Ⓖ Ⓗ Ⓙ
7. Ⓐ Ⓑ Ⓒ Ⓓ
8. Ⓕ Ⓖ Ⓗ Ⓙ
9. Ⓐ Ⓑ Ⓒ Ⓓ
10. Ⓕ Ⓖ Ⓗ Ⓙ

Student Answer Sheets (cont.)

Language Arts: Writing Sample
Test page: 31

_____
_____
_____
_____
_____
_____
_____
_____
_____
_____
_____
_____
_____
_____

Language Arts: Usage
Test page: 30

Samples

A. Ⓐ Ⓑ Ⓒ Ⓓ
B. Ⓕ Ⓖ Ⓗ Ⓙ

Test

1. Ⓐ Ⓑ Ⓒ Ⓓ
2. Ⓕ Ⓖ Ⓗ Ⓙ
3. Ⓐ Ⓑ Ⓒ Ⓓ
4. Ⓕ Ⓖ Ⓗ Ⓙ
5. Ⓐ Ⓑ Ⓒ Ⓓ
6. Ⓕ Ⓖ Ⓗ Ⓙ
7. Ⓐ Ⓑ Ⓒ Ⓓ
8. Ⓕ Ⓖ Ⓗ Ⓙ
9. Ⓐ Ⓑ Ⓒ Ⓓ
10. Ⓕ Ⓖ Ⓗ Ⓙ

Language Arts: Topic Sentences
Test page: 29

Sample

A. Ⓐ Ⓑ Ⓒ Ⓓ

Test

1. Ⓐ Ⓑ Ⓒ Ⓓ
2. Ⓕ Ⓖ Ⓗ Ⓙ
3. Ⓐ Ⓑ Ⓒ Ⓓ

Mathematics: Finding Averages
Test page: 34

Sample

A. Ⓐ Ⓑ Ⓒ Ⓓ

Test

1. Ⓐ Ⓑ Ⓒ Ⓓ
2. Ⓕ Ⓖ Ⓗ Ⓙ
3. Ⓐ Ⓑ Ⓒ Ⓓ
4. Ⓕ Ⓖ Ⓗ Ⓙ
5. Ⓐ Ⓑ Ⓒ Ⓓ
6. Ⓕ Ⓖ Ⓗ Ⓙ

Mathematics: Customary and Metric Units
Test pages: 35–36

Test

1. Ⓐ Ⓑ Ⓒ Ⓓ
2. Ⓕ Ⓖ Ⓗ Ⓙ
3. Ⓐ Ⓑ Ⓒ Ⓓ
4. Ⓕ Ⓖ Ⓗ Ⓙ
5. Ⓐ Ⓑ Ⓒ Ⓓ
6. Ⓕ Ⓖ Ⓗ Ⓙ
7. Ⓐ Ⓑ Ⓒ Ⓓ
8. Ⓕ Ⓖ Ⓗ Ⓙ
9. Ⓐ Ⓑ Ⓒ Ⓓ
10. Ⓕ Ⓖ Ⓗ Ⓙ
11. Ⓐ Ⓑ Ⓒ Ⓓ
12. Ⓕ Ⓖ Ⓗ Ⓙ
13. Ⓐ Ⓑ Ⓒ Ⓓ
14. Ⓕ Ⓖ Ⓗ Ⓙ
15. Ⓐ Ⓑ Ⓒ Ⓓ
16. Ⓕ Ⓖ Ⓗ Ⓙ
17. Ⓐ Ⓑ Ⓒ Ⓓ
18. Ⓕ Ⓖ Ⓗ Ⓙ

Mathematics: Division
Test pages: 37–38

Sample

A. Ⓐ Ⓑ Ⓒ Ⓓ

Test

1. Ⓐ Ⓑ Ⓒ Ⓓ
2. Ⓕ Ⓖ Ⓗ Ⓙ
3. Ⓐ Ⓑ Ⓒ Ⓓ
4. Ⓕ Ⓖ Ⓗ Ⓙ
5. Ⓐ Ⓑ Ⓒ Ⓓ
6. Ⓕ Ⓖ Ⓗ Ⓙ
7. Ⓐ Ⓑ Ⓒ Ⓓ
8. Ⓕ Ⓖ Ⓗ Ⓙ
9. Ⓐ Ⓑ Ⓒ Ⓓ
10. Ⓕ Ⓖ Ⓗ Ⓙ
11. Ⓐ Ⓑ Ⓒ Ⓓ
12. Ⓕ Ⓖ Ⓗ Ⓙ
13. Ⓐ Ⓑ Ⓒ Ⓓ
14. Ⓕ Ⓖ Ⓗ Ⓙ
15. Ⓐ Ⓑ Ⓒ Ⓓ
16. Ⓕ Ⓖ Ⓗ Ⓙ
17. Ⓐ Ⓑ Ⓒ Ⓓ
18. Ⓕ Ⓖ Ⓗ Ⓙ

Mathematics: Fractions—Equivalents and Simplest Terms
Test pages: 39–40

Samples

A. Ⓐ Ⓑ Ⓒ Ⓓ
B. Ⓕ Ⓖ Ⓗ Ⓙ

Test

1. Ⓐ Ⓑ Ⓒ Ⓓ
2. Ⓕ Ⓖ Ⓗ Ⓙ
3. Ⓐ Ⓑ Ⓒ Ⓓ
4. Ⓕ Ⓖ Ⓗ Ⓙ
5. Ⓐ Ⓑ Ⓒ Ⓓ
6. Ⓕ Ⓖ Ⓗ Ⓙ
7. Ⓐ Ⓑ Ⓒ Ⓓ
8. Ⓕ Ⓖ Ⓗ Ⓙ
9. Ⓐ Ⓑ Ⓒ Ⓓ
10. Ⓕ Ⓖ Ⓗ Ⓙ
11. Ⓐ Ⓑ Ⓒ Ⓓ
12. Ⓕ Ⓖ Ⓗ Ⓙ
13. Ⓐ Ⓑ Ⓒ Ⓓ
14. Ⓕ Ⓖ Ⓗ Ⓙ
15. Ⓐ Ⓑ Ⓒ Ⓓ
16. Ⓕ Ⓖ Ⓗ Ⓙ

Student Answer Sheets (cont.)

Mathematics: Factorization
Test pages: 41–42

Samples
A. Ⓐ Ⓑ Ⓒ Ⓓ
B. Ⓕ Ⓖ Ⓗ Ⓙ

Test
1. Ⓐ Ⓑ Ⓒ Ⓓ
2. Ⓕ Ⓖ Ⓗ Ⓙ
3. Ⓐ Ⓑ Ⓒ Ⓓ
4. Ⓕ Ⓖ Ⓗ Ⓙ
5. Ⓐ Ⓑ Ⓒ Ⓓ
6. Ⓕ Ⓖ Ⓗ Ⓙ
7. Ⓐ Ⓑ Ⓒ Ⓓ
8. Ⓕ Ⓖ Ⓗ Ⓙ
9. Ⓐ Ⓑ Ⓒ Ⓓ
10. Ⓕ Ⓖ Ⓗ Ⓙ
11. Ⓐ Ⓑ Ⓒ Ⓓ
12. Ⓕ Ⓖ Ⓗ Ⓙ
13. Ⓐ Ⓑ Ⓒ Ⓓ
14. Ⓕ Ⓖ Ⓗ Ⓙ

Mathematics: Fractions—Adding and Subtracting
Test page: 43

Samples
A. Ⓐ Ⓑ Ⓒ Ⓓ
B. Ⓕ Ⓖ Ⓗ Ⓙ

Test
1. Ⓐ Ⓑ Ⓒ Ⓓ
2. Ⓕ Ⓖ Ⓗ Ⓙ
3. Ⓐ Ⓑ Ⓒ Ⓓ
4. Ⓕ Ⓖ Ⓗ Ⓙ
5. Ⓐ Ⓑ Ⓒ Ⓓ
6. Ⓕ Ⓖ Ⓗ Ⓙ
7. Ⓐ Ⓑ Ⓒ Ⓓ
8. Ⓕ Ⓖ Ⓗ Ⓙ

Mathematics: Geometry
Test pages: 44–45

Sample
A. Ⓐ Ⓑ Ⓒ Ⓓ

Test
1. Ⓐ Ⓑ Ⓒ Ⓓ
2. Ⓕ Ⓖ Ⓗ Ⓙ
3. Ⓐ Ⓑ Ⓒ Ⓓ
4. Ⓕ Ⓖ Ⓗ Ⓙ
5. Ⓐ Ⓑ Ⓒ Ⓓ
6. Ⓕ Ⓖ Ⓗ Ⓙ
7. Ⓐ Ⓑ Ⓒ Ⓓ
8. Ⓕ Ⓖ Ⓗ Ⓙ
9. Ⓐ Ⓑ Ⓒ Ⓓ
10. Ⓕ Ⓖ Ⓗ Ⓙ
11. Ⓐ Ⓑ Ⓒ Ⓓ
12. Ⓕ Ⓖ Ⓗ Ⓙ

Mathematics: Multiplication—Mixed Numbers
Test page: 46

Samples
A. Ⓐ Ⓑ Ⓒ Ⓓ Ⓔ
B. Ⓕ Ⓖ Ⓗ Ⓙ Ⓚ

Test
1. Ⓐ Ⓑ Ⓒ Ⓓ Ⓔ
2. Ⓕ Ⓖ Ⓗ Ⓙ Ⓚ
3. Ⓐ Ⓑ Ⓒ Ⓓ Ⓔ
4. Ⓕ Ⓖ Ⓗ Ⓙ Ⓚ
5. Ⓐ Ⓑ Ⓒ Ⓓ Ⓔ
6. Ⓕ Ⓖ Ⓗ Ⓙ Ⓚ
7. Ⓐ Ⓑ Ⓒ Ⓓ Ⓔ
8. Ⓕ Ⓖ Ⓗ Ⓙ Ⓚ

Student Answer Sheets *(cont.)*

Mathematics: Probability
Test page: 47

Sample

A. Ⓐ Ⓑ Ⓒ Ⓓ

Test

1. Ⓐ Ⓑ Ⓒ Ⓓ
2. Ⓕ Ⓖ Ⓗ Ⓙ
3. Ⓐ Ⓑ Ⓒ Ⓓ
4. Ⓕ Ⓖ Ⓗ Ⓙ
5. Ⓐ Ⓑ Ⓒ Ⓓ
6. Ⓕ Ⓖ Ⓗ Ⓙ

Mathematics: Rounding
Test page: 48

Sample

A. Ⓐ Ⓑ Ⓒ Ⓓ

Test

1. Ⓐ Ⓑ Ⓒ Ⓓ
2. Ⓕ Ⓖ Ⓗ Ⓙ
3. Ⓐ Ⓑ Ⓒ Ⓓ
4. Ⓕ Ⓖ Ⓗ Ⓙ
5. Ⓐ Ⓑ Ⓒ Ⓓ
6. Ⓕ Ⓖ Ⓗ Ⓙ
7. Ⓐ Ⓑ Ⓒ Ⓓ
8. Ⓕ Ⓖ Ⓗ Ⓙ

Mathematics: Operations with Whole Numbers
Test pages: 49–50

Samples

A. Ⓐ Ⓑ Ⓒ Ⓓ Ⓔ
B. Ⓕ Ⓖ Ⓗ Ⓙ Ⓚ

Test

1. Ⓐ Ⓑ Ⓒ Ⓓ Ⓔ
2. Ⓕ Ⓖ Ⓗ Ⓙ Ⓚ
3. Ⓐ Ⓑ Ⓒ Ⓓ Ⓔ
4. Ⓕ Ⓖ Ⓗ Ⓙ Ⓚ
5. Ⓐ Ⓑ Ⓒ Ⓓ Ⓔ
6. Ⓕ Ⓖ Ⓗ Ⓙ Ⓚ
7. Ⓐ Ⓑ Ⓒ Ⓓ Ⓔ
8. Ⓕ Ⓖ Ⓗ Ⓙ Ⓚ
9. Ⓐ Ⓑ Ⓒ Ⓓ Ⓔ
10. Ⓕ Ⓖ Ⓗ Ⓙ Ⓚ
11. Ⓐ Ⓑ Ⓒ Ⓓ Ⓔ
12. Ⓕ Ⓖ Ⓗ Ⓙ Ⓚ
13. Ⓐ Ⓑ Ⓒ Ⓓ Ⓔ
14. Ⓕ Ⓖ Ⓗ Ⓙ Ⓚ
15. Ⓐ Ⓑ Ⓒ Ⓓ Ⓔ
16. Ⓕ Ⓖ Ⓗ Ⓙ Ⓚ
17. Ⓐ Ⓑ Ⓒ Ⓓ Ⓔ
18. Ⓕ Ⓖ Ⓗ Ⓙ Ⓚ
19. Ⓐ Ⓑ Ⓒ Ⓓ Ⓔ
20. Ⓕ Ⓖ Ⓗ Ⓙ Ⓚ

Science: Earth Science
Test pages: 53–54

Sample

A. Ⓐ Ⓑ Ⓒ Ⓓ Ⓔ

Test

1. Ⓐ Ⓑ Ⓒ Ⓓ Ⓔ
2. Ⓕ Ⓖ Ⓗ Ⓙ Ⓚ
3. Ⓐ Ⓑ Ⓒ Ⓓ Ⓔ
4. Ⓕ Ⓖ Ⓗ Ⓙ Ⓚ
5. Ⓐ Ⓑ Ⓒ Ⓓ Ⓔ
6. Ⓕ Ⓖ Ⓗ Ⓙ Ⓚ
7. Ⓐ Ⓑ Ⓒ Ⓓ Ⓔ
8. Ⓕ Ⓖ Ⓗ Ⓙ Ⓚ
9. Ⓐ Ⓑ Ⓒ Ⓓ Ⓔ
10. Ⓕ Ⓖ Ⓗ Ⓙ Ⓚ
11. Ⓐ Ⓑ Ⓒ Ⓓ Ⓔ
12. Ⓕ Ⓖ Ⓗ Ⓙ Ⓚ
13. Ⓐ Ⓑ Ⓒ Ⓓ Ⓔ
14. Ⓕ Ⓖ Ⓗ Ⓙ Ⓚ
15. Ⓐ Ⓑ Ⓒ Ⓓ Ⓔ
16. Ⓕ Ⓖ Ⓗ Ⓙ Ⓚ
17. Ⓐ Ⓑ Ⓒ Ⓓ Ⓔ
18. Ⓕ Ⓖ Ⓗ Ⓙ Ⓚ

Student Answer Sheets *(cont.)*

Science: Physical Science
Test pages: 58–59

Sample

A. Ⓐ Ⓑ Ⓒ Ⓓ

Test

1. Ⓐ Ⓑ Ⓒ Ⓓ
2. Ⓕ Ⓖ Ⓗ Ⓙ
3. Ⓐ Ⓑ Ⓒ Ⓓ
4. Ⓕ Ⓖ Ⓗ Ⓙ
5. Ⓐ Ⓑ Ⓒ Ⓓ
6. Ⓕ Ⓖ Ⓗ Ⓙ
7. Ⓐ Ⓑ Ⓒ Ⓓ
8. Ⓕ Ⓖ Ⓗ Ⓙ
9. Ⓐ Ⓑ Ⓒ Ⓓ
10. Ⓕ Ⓖ Ⓗ Ⓙ
11. Ⓐ Ⓑ Ⓒ Ⓓ
12. Ⓕ Ⓖ Ⓗ Ⓙ
13. Ⓐ Ⓑ Ⓒ Ⓓ
14. Ⓕ Ⓖ Ⓗ Ⓙ
15. Ⓐ Ⓑ Ⓒ Ⓓ
16. Ⓕ Ⓖ Ⓗ Ⓙ
17. Ⓐ Ⓑ Ⓒ Ⓓ
18. Ⓕ Ⓖ Ⓗ Ⓙ

Science: Invertebrates
Test page: 57

Sample

A. Ⓐ Ⓑ Ⓒ Ⓓ

Test

1. Ⓐ Ⓑ Ⓒ Ⓓ
2. Ⓕ Ⓖ Ⓗ Ⓙ
3. Ⓐ Ⓑ Ⓒ Ⓓ
4. Ⓕ Ⓖ Ⓗ Ⓙ
5. Ⓐ Ⓑ Ⓒ Ⓓ
6. Ⓕ Ⓖ Ⓗ Ⓙ
7. Ⓐ Ⓑ Ⓒ Ⓓ
8. Ⓕ Ⓖ Ⓗ Ⓙ
9. Ⓐ Ⓑ Ⓒ Ⓓ
10. Ⓕ Ⓖ Ⓗ Ⓙ

Science: The Human Body
Test page: 56

Sample

A. Ⓐ Ⓑ Ⓒ Ⓓ Ⓔ

Test

1. Ⓐ Ⓑ Ⓒ Ⓓ Ⓔ
2. Ⓕ Ⓖ Ⓗ Ⓙ Ⓚ
3. Ⓐ Ⓑ Ⓒ Ⓓ Ⓔ
4. Ⓕ Ⓖ Ⓗ Ⓙ Ⓚ
5. Ⓐ Ⓑ Ⓒ Ⓓ Ⓔ
6. Ⓕ Ⓖ Ⓗ Ⓙ Ⓚ
7. Ⓐ Ⓑ Ⓒ Ⓓ Ⓔ
8. Ⓕ Ⓖ Ⓗ Ⓙ Ⓚ
9. Ⓐ Ⓑ Ⓒ Ⓓ Ⓔ
10. Ⓕ Ⓖ Ⓗ Ⓙ Ⓚ

Science: Electricity and Magnetism
Test page: 55

Test

1. Ⓐ Ⓑ Ⓒ Ⓓ
2. Ⓕ Ⓖ Ⓗ Ⓙ
3. Ⓐ Ⓑ Ⓒ Ⓓ
4. Ⓕ Ⓖ Ⓗ Ⓙ
5. Ⓐ Ⓑ Ⓒ Ⓓ
6. Ⓕ Ⓖ Ⓗ Ⓙ
7. Ⓐ Ⓑ Ⓒ Ⓓ
8. Ⓕ Ⓖ Ⓗ Ⓙ
9. Ⓐ Ⓑ Ⓒ Ⓓ
10. Ⓕ Ⓖ Ⓗ Ⓙ

Science: The Solar System
Test page: 64

Test

1. (A) (B) (C) (D)
2. (F) (G) (H) (J)
3. (A) (B) (C) (D)
4. (F) (G) (H) (J)
5. (A) (B) (C) (D)
6. (F) (G) (H) (J)
7. (A) (B) (C) (D)
8. (F) (G) (H) (J)
9. (A) (B) (C) (D)
10. (F) (G) (H) (J)

Science: Simple Organisms
Test page: 63

Sample

A. (A) (B) (C) (D) (E)

Test

1. (A) (B) (C) (D) (E)
2. (A) (B) (C) (D) (E)
3. (A) (B) (C) (D) (E)
4. (A) (B) (C) (D) (E)
5. (F) (G) (H) (J) (K)
6. (F) (G) (H) (J) (K)
7. (F) (G) (H) (J) (K)
8. (F) (G) (H) (J) (K)
9. (F) (G) (H) (J) (K)
10. (F) (G) (H) (J) (K)
11. (A) (B) (C) (D) (E)
12. (F) (G) (H) (J) (K)

Science Reading: Earthquakes
Test pages: 61–62

Test

1. (A) (B) (C) (D) (E)
2. (F) (G) (H) (J) (K)
3. (A) (B) (C) (D) (E)
4. (F) (G) (H) (J) (K)
5. (A) (B) (C) (D) (E)
6. (F) (G) (H) (J) (K)
7. (A) (B) (C) (D) (E)
8. (F) (G) (H) (J) (K)
9. (A) (B) (C) (D) (E)
10. (F) (G) (H) (J) (K)

Science Reading: Fossils
Test page: 60

Test

1. (A) (B) (C) (D)
2. (F) (G) (H) (J)
3. (A) (B) (C) (D)
4. (F) (G) (H) (J)
5. (A) (B) (C) (D)
6. (F) (G) (H) (J)

Student Answer Sheets *(cont.)*

Social Studies: Terms
Test page: 67

Test

1.	A	B	C	D
2.	A	B	C	D
3.	A	B	C	D
4.	A	B	C	D
5.	F	G	H	J
6.	F	G	H	J
7.	F	G	H	J
8.	F	G	H	J
9.	A	B	C	D
10.	A	B	C	D
11.	A	B	C	D
12.	A	B	C	D
13.	F	G	H	J
14.	F	G	H	J
15.	F	G	H	J
16.	F	G	H	J

Social Studies: Sequencing
Test page: 68

Sample

A. A B C D

Test

1.	A	B	C	D
2.	F	G	H	J
3.	A	B	C	D
4.	F	G	H	J
5.	A	B	C	D
6.	F	G	H	J

Social Studies: Famous Persons
Test page: 69

Sample

A. A B C D

Test

1.	A	B	C	D
2.	F	G	H	J
3.	A	B	C	D
4.	F	G	H	J
5.	A	B	C	D
6.	F	G	H	J
7.	A	B	C	D
8.	F	G	H	J
9.	A	B	C	D
10.	F	G	H	J

Social Studies: Famous Places
Test page: 70

Sample

A. A B C D

Test

1.	A	B	C	D
2.	F	G	H	J
3.	A	B	C	D
4.	F	G	H	J
5.	A	B	C	D
6.	F	G	H	J
7.	A	B	C	D
8.	F	G	H	J
9.	A	B	C	D
10.	F	G	H	J

Student Answer Sheets (cont.)

Social Studies: Maps and Globes
Test page: 71

Samples

A. Ⓐ Ⓑ Ⓒ Ⓓ
B. Ⓕ Ⓖ Ⓗ Ⓙ

Test

1. Ⓐ Ⓑ Ⓒ Ⓓ
2. Ⓕ Ⓖ Ⓗ Ⓙ
3. Ⓐ Ⓑ Ⓒ Ⓓ
4. Ⓕ Ⓖ Ⓗ Ⓙ
5. Ⓐ Ⓑ Ⓒ Ⓓ
6. Ⓕ Ⓖ Ⓗ Ⓙ
7. Ⓐ Ⓑ Ⓒ Ⓓ
8. Ⓕ Ⓖ Ⓗ Ⓙ
9. Ⓐ Ⓑ Ⓒ Ⓓ
10. Ⓕ Ⓖ Ⓗ Ⓙ
11. Ⓐ Ⓑ Ⓒ Ⓓ
12. Ⓕ Ⓖ Ⓗ Ⓙ

Social Studies: United States History
Test pages: 72–73

Test

1. Ⓐ Ⓑ Ⓒ Ⓓ Ⓔ
2. Ⓕ Ⓖ Ⓗ Ⓙ Ⓚ
3. Ⓐ Ⓑ Ⓒ Ⓓ Ⓔ
4. Ⓕ Ⓖ Ⓗ Ⓙ Ⓚ
5. Ⓐ Ⓑ Ⓒ Ⓓ Ⓔ
6. Ⓕ Ⓖ Ⓗ Ⓙ Ⓚ
7. Ⓐ Ⓑ Ⓒ Ⓓ Ⓔ
8. Ⓕ Ⓖ Ⓗ Ⓙ Ⓚ
9. Ⓐ Ⓑ Ⓒ Ⓓ Ⓔ
10. Ⓕ Ⓖ Ⓗ Ⓙ Ⓚ
11. Ⓐ Ⓑ Ⓒ Ⓓ Ⓔ
12. Ⓕ Ⓖ Ⓗ Ⓙ Ⓚ

Social Studies: Reading Comprehension
Test pages: 74–75

Test

1. Ⓐ Ⓑ Ⓒ Ⓓ
2. Ⓕ Ⓖ Ⓗ Ⓙ
3. Ⓐ Ⓑ Ⓒ Ⓓ
4. Ⓕ Ⓖ Ⓗ Ⓙ
5. Ⓐ Ⓑ Ⓒ Ⓓ
6. Ⓕ Ⓖ Ⓗ Ⓙ

Social Studies: Concepts
Test page: 76

Test

1. Ⓐ Ⓑ Ⓒ Ⓓ Ⓔ
2. Ⓕ Ⓖ Ⓗ Ⓙ Ⓚ
3. Ⓐ Ⓑ Ⓒ Ⓓ Ⓔ
4. Ⓕ Ⓖ Ⓗ Ⓙ Ⓚ
5. Ⓐ Ⓑ Ⓒ Ⓓ Ⓔ
6. Ⓕ Ⓖ Ⓗ Ⓙ Ⓚ
7. Ⓐ Ⓑ Ⓒ Ⓓ Ⓔ
8. Ⓕ Ⓖ Ⓗ Ⓙ Ⓚ
9. Ⓐ Ⓑ Ⓒ Ⓓ Ⓔ
10. Ⓕ Ⓖ Ⓗ Ⓙ Ⓚ

Language Arts: Synonym Analogies
Test page: 17

Sample

A. Ⓐ **⬤** Ⓒ Ⓓ

Test

1. Ⓐ Ⓑ **⬤** Ⓓ
2. Ⓕ Ⓖ Ⓗ **⬤**
3. Ⓐ **⬤** Ⓒ Ⓓ
4. Ⓕ Ⓖ Ⓗ **⬤**
5. Ⓐ **⬤** Ⓒ Ⓓ
6. Ⓕ Ⓖ **⬤** Ⓙ
7. Ⓐ Ⓑ Ⓒ **⬤**
8. Ⓕ Ⓖ Ⓗ **⬤**

Language Arts: Capitalization
Test page: 18

Samples

A. Ⓐ Ⓑ Ⓒ **⬤**
B. **⬤** Ⓖ Ⓗ Ⓙ

Test

1. Ⓐ Ⓑ **⬤** Ⓓ
2. Ⓕ Ⓖ Ⓗ **⬤**
3. Ⓐ Ⓑ **⬤** Ⓓ
4. Ⓕ **⬤** Ⓗ Ⓙ
5. Ⓐ Ⓑ Ⓒ **⬤**
6. **⬤** Ⓖ Ⓗ Ⓙ
7. Ⓐ Ⓑ **⬤** Ⓓ
8. **⬤** Ⓖ Ⓗ Ⓙ

Language Arts: Fiction
Test pages: 19–21

Test

1. Ⓐ **⬤** Ⓒ Ⓓ
2. Ⓕ **⬤** Ⓗ Ⓙ
3. Ⓐ Ⓑ Ⓒ **⬤**
4. Ⓕ Ⓖ **⬤** Ⓙ
5. Ⓐ **⬤** Ⓒ Ⓓ
6. Ⓕ Ⓖ Ⓗ **⬤**
7. Ⓐ Ⓑ Ⓒ **⬤**
8. Ⓕ Ⓖ **⬤** Ⓙ

Language Arts: Poetry and Verse
Test pages: 22–23

Test

1. Ⓐ **⬤** Ⓒ Ⓓ
2. Ⓕ Ⓖ **⬤** Ⓙ
3. **⬤** Ⓑ Ⓒ Ⓓ
4. Ⓕ **⬤** Ⓗ Ⓙ
5. Ⓐ Ⓑ Ⓒ **⬤**
6. Ⓕ Ⓖ **⬤** Ⓙ
7. Student responses will vary. Responses are to be evaluated by the teacher.
8. Student responses will vary. Responses are to be evaluated by the teacher.
9. Ⓐ Ⓑ **⬤** Ⓓ
10. Student responses will vary. Responses are to be evaluated by the teacher.

Language Arts: Punctuation — Test page: 24

Sample
A. D

Test
1. D
2. J
3. D
4. H
5. D
6. J

Language Arts: Research — Test pages: 25–26

Test
1. B
2. F
3. B
4. J
5. B
6. H
7. B
8. G
9. B
10. F
11. B
12. F
13. C
14. H
15. A
16. F

Language Arts: Sentences — Test page: 27

Sample
A. B

Test
1. B
2. H
3. B
4. H

Language Arts: Spelling — Test page: 28

Samples
A. C
B. J

Test
1. B
2. F
3. C
4. J
5. A
6. G
7. B
8. G
9. B
10. J

Language Arts: Topic Sentences
Test page: 29

Sample

A. Ⓐ ● Ⓒ Ⓓ

Test

1. Ⓐ Ⓑ ● Ⓓ
2. Ⓕ ● Ⓗ Ⓙ
3. Ⓐ Ⓑ ● Ⓓ

Language Arts: Usage
Test page: 30

Samples

A. Ⓐ ● Ⓒ Ⓓ
B. Ⓕ Ⓖ Ⓗ ●

Test

1. Ⓐ Ⓑ ● Ⓓ
2. Ⓕ ● Ⓗ Ⓙ
3. Ⓐ Ⓑ ● Ⓓ
4. Ⓕ ● Ⓗ Ⓙ
5. ● Ⓑ Ⓒ Ⓓ
6. Ⓕ Ⓖ Ⓗ ●
7. ● Ⓑ Ⓒ Ⓓ
8. ● Ⓖ Ⓗ Ⓙ
9. Ⓐ ● Ⓒ Ⓓ
10. Ⓕ ● Ⓗ Ⓙ

Language Arts: Writing Sample
Test page: 31

Student responses will vary. Responses are to be evaluated by the teacher.

Mathematics: Fractions—Equivalents and Simplest Terms
Test pages: 39–40

Samples

	A/F	B/G	C/H	D/J
A.	●	Ⓑ	Ⓒ	Ⓓ
B.	●	Ⓖ	Ⓗ	Ⓙ

Test

	A/F	B/G	C/H	D/J
1.	Ⓐ	Ⓑ	●	Ⓓ
2.	Ⓕ	Ⓖ	●	Ⓙ
3.	Ⓐ	●	Ⓒ	Ⓓ
4.	Ⓕ	Ⓖ	●	Ⓙ
5.	Ⓐ	●	Ⓒ	Ⓓ
6.	Ⓕ	●	Ⓗ	Ⓙ
7.	Ⓐ	Ⓖ	●	Ⓙ
8.	●	Ⓖ	Ⓗ	Ⓙ
9.	Ⓐ	Ⓑ	Ⓒ	●
10.	Ⓕ	●	Ⓗ	Ⓙ
11.	Ⓐ	Ⓖ	●	Ⓙ
12.	●	Ⓖ	Ⓗ	Ⓙ
13.	Ⓐ	Ⓑ	●	●
14.	Ⓕ	●	Ⓗ	Ⓙ
15.	Ⓐ	Ⓖ	Ⓒ	●
16.	●	Ⓖ	Ⓗ	Ⓙ

Mathematics: Division
Test pages: 37–38

Sample

	A	B	C	D
A.	Ⓐ	Ⓑ	●	●

Test

	A/F	B/G	C/H	D/J
1.	Ⓐ	Ⓑ	●	Ⓓ
2.	Ⓕ	●	Ⓗ	Ⓙ
3.	Ⓐ	Ⓑ	Ⓒ	●
4.	●	Ⓖ	Ⓗ	Ⓙ
5.	●	Ⓑ	Ⓗ	Ⓓ
6.	Ⓕ	●	●	Ⓙ
7.	Ⓐ	Ⓑ	Ⓒ	Ⓓ
8.	Ⓕ	Ⓖ	●	Ⓙ
9.	Ⓐ	Ⓑ	Ⓗ	Ⓓ
10.	Ⓕ	●	Ⓒ	Ⓙ
11.	Ⓐ	●	Ⓗ	Ⓓ
12.	Ⓕ	Ⓖ	Ⓒ	Ⓙ
13.	●	Ⓑ	●	Ⓓ
14.	Ⓕ	Ⓑ	●	Ⓓ
15.	Ⓐ	Ⓑ	Ⓒ	Ⓓ
16.	Ⓕ	Ⓖ	●	Ⓓ
17.	Ⓐ	●	Ⓗ	Ⓓ
18.	Ⓕ	Ⓖ	●	●

Mathematics: Customary and Metric Units
Test pages: 35–36

Test

	A/F	B/G	C/H	D/J
1.	●	Ⓑ	Ⓒ	Ⓓ
2.	●	Ⓖ	Ⓗ	Ⓙ
3.	●	Ⓑ	Ⓒ	Ⓓ
4.	Ⓕ	Ⓖ	●	Ⓙ
5.	Ⓐ	Ⓑ	Ⓒ	●
6.	Ⓕ	●	Ⓗ	Ⓙ
7.	Ⓐ	Ⓑ	Ⓒ	Ⓓ
8.	Ⓕ	Ⓖ	Ⓗ	Ⓙ
9.	Ⓐ	Ⓑ	Ⓒ	●
10.	Ⓕ	Ⓖ	Ⓗ	●
11.	Ⓐ	Ⓑ	Ⓒ	●
12.	Ⓕ	●	●	Ⓙ
13.	Ⓐ	●	Ⓒ	Ⓓ
14.	Ⓕ	Ⓖ	Ⓒ	Ⓙ
15.	●	Ⓑ	Ⓒ	Ⓓ
16.	●	Ⓖ	Ⓒ	Ⓓ
17.	Ⓐ	Ⓑ	Ⓗ	Ⓙ
18.	Ⓕ	Ⓖ	●	Ⓙ

Mathematics: Finding Averages
Test page: 34

Sample

	A	B	C	D
A.	Ⓐ	●	Ⓒ	Ⓓ

Test

	A/F	B/G	C/H	D/J
1.	Ⓐ	Ⓑ	●	Ⓓ
2.	Ⓕ	Ⓖ	●	●
3.	Ⓐ	●	Ⓒ	Ⓓ
4.	Ⓕ	●	Ⓗ	Ⓙ
5.	Ⓐ	Ⓑ	●	●
6.	Ⓕ	Ⓖ	Ⓗ	●

Mathematics: Factorization
Test pages: 41–42

Samples
- A. B
- B. J

Test
1	2	3	4	5	6	7	8	9	10	11	12	13	14
C	H	A	J	B	G	D	H	C	G	B	F	A	J

Mathematics: Fractions—Adding and Subtracting
Test page: 43

Samples
- A. D
- B. F

Test
1	2	3	4	5	6	7	8
D	F	A	G	C	J	D	G

Mathematics: Geometry
Test pages: 44–45

Sample
- A. B

Test
1	2	3	4	5	6	7	8	9	10	11	12
C	G	D	H	B	F	C	H	C	H	D	H

Mathematics: Multiplication—Mixed Numbers
Test page: 46

Samples
- A. D
- B. G

Test
1	2	3	4	5	6	7	8
D	H	D	K	A	J	B	G

Answer Key *(cont.)*

Science: Earth Science
Test pages: 53–54

Sample

	A	B	C	D	E
A.	●	Ⓑ	Ⓒ	Ⓓ	Ⓔ

Test

#	A/F	B/G	C/H	D/J	E/K
1.	●	Ⓑ	Ⓒ	Ⓓ	Ⓔ
2.	●	Ⓖ	Ⓗ	Ⓙ	Ⓚ
3.	Ⓐ	●	Ⓒ	Ⓓ	Ⓔ
4.	Ⓕ	●	Ⓗ	Ⓙ	Ⓚ
5.	Ⓐ	Ⓑ	Ⓒ	●	Ⓔ
6.	Ⓕ	Ⓖ	Ⓗ	●	Ⓚ
7.	●	Ⓑ	Ⓒ	Ⓓ	Ⓔ
8.	Ⓕ	Ⓖ	Ⓗ	●	Ⓚ
9.	Ⓐ	Ⓑ	Ⓒ	●	Ⓔ
10.	Ⓕ	Ⓖ	Ⓗ	●	Ⓚ
11.	Ⓐ	Ⓑ	●	Ⓓ	Ⓔ
12.	Ⓕ	●	Ⓗ	Ⓙ	Ⓚ
13.	Ⓐ	●	Ⓒ	Ⓓ	Ⓔ
14.	Ⓕ	Ⓖ	●	Ⓙ	Ⓚ
15.	●	Ⓑ	Ⓒ	Ⓓ	Ⓔ
16.	●	Ⓖ	Ⓗ	Ⓙ	Ⓚ
17.	Ⓐ	Ⓑ	●	Ⓓ	Ⓔ
18.	Ⓕ	Ⓖ	Ⓗ	Ⓙ	●

Mathematics: Operations with Whole Numbers
Test pages: 49–50

Samples

	A/F	B/G	C/H	D/J	E/K
A.	Ⓐ	Ⓑ	Ⓒ	Ⓓ	●
B.	Ⓕ	●	Ⓗ	Ⓙ	Ⓚ

Test

#	A/F	B/G	C/H	D/J	E/K
1.	●	Ⓑ	Ⓒ	Ⓓ	Ⓔ
2.	Ⓕ	●	Ⓗ	Ⓙ	Ⓚ
3.	●	Ⓖ	Ⓒ	Ⓓ	Ⓔ
4.	●	Ⓑ	Ⓗ	Ⓙ	Ⓚ
5.	Ⓐ	Ⓑ	Ⓒ	Ⓓ	●
6.	Ⓕ	●	Ⓗ	Ⓙ	Ⓚ
7.	●	Ⓑ	Ⓒ	Ⓓ	Ⓔ
8.	Ⓕ	●	Ⓗ	Ⓙ	Ⓚ
9.	Ⓐ	Ⓖ	●	Ⓓ	Ⓔ
10.	Ⓕ	Ⓑ	Ⓗ	Ⓙ	●
11.	●	Ⓑ	Ⓒ	Ⓓ	Ⓔ
12.	Ⓕ	●	Ⓗ	Ⓙ	Ⓚ
13.	Ⓐ	Ⓑ	●	Ⓓ	Ⓔ
14.	Ⓕ	Ⓖ	●	Ⓙ	Ⓚ
15.	●	Ⓑ	Ⓒ	Ⓓ	Ⓔ
16.	Ⓕ	Ⓖ	Ⓗ	●	Ⓚ
17.	Ⓐ	Ⓑ	●	Ⓓ	Ⓔ
18.	Ⓕ	●	Ⓗ	Ⓙ	Ⓚ
19.	Ⓐ	●	Ⓒ	Ⓓ	Ⓔ
20.	●	Ⓖ	Ⓗ	Ⓙ	Ⓚ

Mathematics: Rounding
Test page: 48

Sample

	A	B	C	D
A.	Ⓐ	Ⓑ	●	Ⓓ

Test

#	A/F	B/G	C/H	D/J
1.	●	Ⓑ	Ⓒ	Ⓓ
2.	Ⓕ	●	Ⓗ	Ⓙ
3.	Ⓐ	●	Ⓒ	Ⓓ
4.	Ⓕ	●	Ⓗ	Ⓙ
5.	●	Ⓑ	Ⓒ	Ⓓ
6.	Ⓕ	●	Ⓗ	Ⓙ
7.	Ⓐ	Ⓑ	Ⓒ	●
8.	Ⓕ	Ⓖ	●	Ⓙ

Mathematics: Probability
Test page: 47

Sample

	A	B	C	D
A.	Ⓐ	Ⓑ	●	Ⓓ

Test

#	A/F	B/G	C/H	D/J
1.	Ⓐ	●	Ⓒ	Ⓓ
2.	Ⓕ	●	Ⓗ	Ⓙ
3.	Ⓐ	●	Ⓒ	Ⓓ
4.	Ⓕ	Ⓖ	●	Ⓙ
5.	Ⓐ	●	Ⓒ	Ⓓ
6.	Ⓕ	●	Ⓗ	Ⓙ

Answer Key (cont.)

Science: Physical Science
Test pages: 58–59

Sample
A. Ⓐ Ⓑ Ⓒ ●

Test
#	Answer
1.	D
2.	F
3.	G
4.	H
5.	G
6.	G
7.	G
8.	H
9.	G
10.	J
11.	H
12.	H
13.	H
14.	J
15.	G
16.	H
17.	H
18.	G

Science: Invertebrates
Test page: 57

Sample
A. Ⓐ ● Ⓒ Ⓓ

Test
#	Answer
1.	B
2.	G
3.	B
4.	J
5.	B
6.	J
7.	B
8.	J
9.	B
10.	J

Science: The Human Body
Test page: 56

Sample
A. ● Ⓑ Ⓒ Ⓓ Ⓔ

Test
#	Answer
1.	C
2.	F
3.	C
4.	H
5.	B
6.	H
7.	B
8.	H
9.	B
10.	C

Science: Electricity and Magnetism
Test page: 55

Test
#	Answer
1.	A
2.	H
3.	H
4.	G
5.	H
6.	G
7.	G
8.	G
9.	A
10.	H

Answer Key (cont.)

Science: The Solar System
Test page: 64

Test

1.	B
2.	H
3.	D
4.	G
5.	B
6.	H
7.	D
8.	G
9.	B
10.	J

Science: Simple Organisms
Test page: 63

Sample

A.	A

Test

1.	D
2.	E
3.	B
4.	G
5.	A
6.	H
7.	J
8.	K
9.	A
10.	G
11.	D
12.	G

Science Reading: Earthquakes
Test pages: 61–62

Test

1.	D
2.	H
3.	F
4.	G
5.	F
6.	H
7.	G
8.	H
9.	G
10.	G

Science Reading: Fossils
Test page: 60

Test

1.	A
2.	J
3.	A
4.	G
5.	H
6.	H

Social Studies: Terms
Test page: 67

Test

#	Answer
1.	B
2.	J
3.	F
4.	H
5.	H
6.	J
7.	F
8.	G
9.	J
10.	F
11.	H
12.	G
13.	D
14.	G
15.	H
16.	F

Social Studies: Sequencing
Test page: 68

Sample

A. D

Test

#	Answer
1.	B
2.	J
3.	H
4.	G
5.	J
6.	G

Social Studies: Famous Persons
Test page: 69

Sample

A. A

Test

#	Answer
1.	D
2.	G
3.	G
4.	J
5.	F
6.	G
7.	J
8.	G
9.	F
10.	F

Social Studies: Famous Places
Test page: 70

Sample

A. C

Test

#	Answer
1.	B
2.	H
3.	F
4.	J
5.	B
6.	J
7.	F
8.	G
9.	B
10.	J

Answer Key *(cont.)*

Social Studies: Maps and Globes
Test page: 71

Samples

A. B
B. G

Test

#	Answer
1.	C
2.	G
3.	A
4.	J
5.	B
6.	J
7.	C
8.	H
9.	B
10.	G
11.	A
12.	G

Social Studies: United States History
Test pages: 72–73

Test

#	Answer
1.	D
2.	J
3.	D
4.	J
5.	B
6.	F
7.	A
8.	J
9.	A
10.	G
11.	B
12.	J

Social Studies: Reading Comprehension
Test pages: 74–75

Test

#	Answer
1.	A
2.	H
3.	B
4.	G
5.	A
6.	H

Social Studies: Concepts
Test page: 76

Test

#	Answer
1.	B
2.	K
3.	C
4.	G
5.	A
6.	J
7.	E
8.	H
9.	D
10.	F